It was so great ~ work with you in Shelby! You were a great spiritual leader for our group & I really hope you enjoy this book & share it with your friends + church!

The Gospel According to
ROCK!

Peace

Toby Jones

Books & Bridges
Harbor Springs, Michigan

Published by Books & Bridges, LLC
2640 Quick Road
Harbor Springs, MI 49740

Publisher's Cataloging-in-Publication Data
Jones, Toby

The gospel according to rock / Toby Jones. – Harbor Springs, MI : Books & Bridges, LLC, 2007.

p. ; cm.
Summary: Long considered "the devil's music," secular rock-n-roll may actually help us hear the voice of God.

ISBN: 978-0-9797793-0-5

1. Rock music—History and criticism. 2. Rock music—Religious aspects. I. Title.

ML3534 .J66 2007
781.66/--dc22   2007931864

Project coordination by Jenkins Group, Inc • *www.BookPublishing.com*

Printed in the United States of America
11 10 09 08 07 • 5 4 3 2 1

Dedication

This book is dedicated to my grandmother, Doris Bailey Baker, and to my mother, Joyce Bailey Jones. Both of these amazing women passed away in the last few years, but not before they gave me the most important gifts there are: faith, hope, love, music, and a deep appreciation for language.

Contents

Acknowledgments

G.W. & Joyce Jones — my parents, who made music a part of my life from day one!

Jeff & Steve Jones — my blood brothers who introduced me to great rock-n-roll, if only through the closed, locked doors of their bedrooms. (I guess I can tell you now that I used to sneak your LP's out of your rooms when you weren't around.)

Jamie and Will Shier — my sister and brother-in-law, who gave me helpful criticism and lots of song ideas. Thanks for proofreading this down the stretch, Jame!

All the musicians whose work is in this book. You've consistently rocked my spiritual world and brought me immeasurable joy!

David Crouse — my brother from a different mother and my Barnabas.

Chip Duncan — for living a life that inspires me and for offering your expertise, passion, and encouragement.

Margaret Lund of The Cook & Franke S.C. Law Firm in Milwaukee for your terrific help getting me started.

Copland Rudolph — the best spinning instructor in the world. The idea for this book came while you were kicking my butt in your class.

Kate Bassett — my earliest and most frequent reader, my constant encourager and friend, and, most recently, my proofreader.

Patrick Nagi — for sharing the writer's journey with me and for getting me the discount!

The Coveralls — my favorite band, for the chance to perform so many of these songs in Cleveland — the rock-n-roll capital of the world!

The First Presbyterian Church of Harbor Springs — for supporting me, my music, and my writing.

Connie Fisher — who read several drafts of this and helped my dream of having my book on sale at my favorite bookstore — Mclean & Eakin Booksellers — come true!

The Jenkins Group — for taking my manuscript and turning it into such a beautiful book. Thanks for mypubsite.com as well.

David and Caroline McCarthy — for a great cover and the best picture of me anyone has ever taken! (That air brush is amazing! Can you give me some hair next time?)

Brian McLaren & Rob Bell — your exciting theology has freed me to get out of the box.

Molly Jones — my wife and muse — and Miles & Liza — our kids — for your patience with me through all the hours I spent writing this thing.

God — for being so much BIGGER than any of us can ever imagine. Despite what Barry Manilow may have thought, YOU are music and YOU write the songs!

Author's Note

While I have been performing rock music for more than thirty years, I make no claim to speak for any of the artists or songwriters whose work I analyze and interpret in this collection. Not having had the opportunity to interview any of the songwriters referenced here — though I hope to someday — I do not presume to know their intentions. But as a long-time writer, I learned very early on that once a work of art is presented to the public, it takes on a life of its own — a life not necessarily in line with the artist's intent. Even in college, I remember turning my short stories over to the 12 other writers in my senior seminar for their review. Listening to what my colleagues saw in my work was an eye-opening experience. Invariably, I would think, "I wasn't attempting to do that," or "that's not what I meant, but I guess I can see where she got that idea." The enduring lesson from my lifetime of writing is that once we submit our work to the public, it is no longer ours and we will have no control of what readers take from it. While this truth is disconcerting to many writers, I have come to revel in the fact that our artistic productions are, in a very real sense, bigger than we are, bigger even than our intentions. My careful, thorough, and respectful treatment of the more than one hundred rock songs referenced in this work is my tribute both to the greatness of the artists and the greatness of the God who inspired them.

The Gospel According to Rock is purely my theological reflection upon their works. My hope is that my reflection will inspire yours.

I believe that whenever we assume God can speak only through those channels typically thought of as religious, we limit God and disregard the witness of both Old and New Testaments. Many of Jesus' most contentious exchanges with the religious leaders of his day grew out of their refusal to believe that God not only associates with sinners, tax collectors, and the non-religious, but even speaks through them from time to time.

Introduction

It was 1977. I was 15 years old, barricaded in the basement, and playing the Beatles' White album backwards over and over, with the volume as loud as it would go. It was a retaliatory gesture aimed at my mother, who had come home from Bible study that day and confiscated my KISS Alive II album, because our pastor had convinced her that KISS stood for "Knights in Satan's Service." If allowed to listen to the "devil's music," mom parroted, it would only be a matter of time before I'd be biting off the heads of bats and contemplating suicide.

My mother wasn't the only person freaked out by rock's corrupting capability. I remember when Black Sabbath was blamed for the suicide of a teen the band didn't even know, and when Alice Cooper was accused of conducting satanic animal sacrifices on stage. Even before these 'real life' events hit the news, rock stars had terrified millions of parents with their hedonistic lifestyles and their profanity-laced lyrics. It's no wonder by the mid-70's the religious establishment had come to associate all things rock with the devil himself.

But despite these fears and protestations, rock hasn't gone away. As Neil Young put it, "Hey, hey, my, my, Rock-n-roll will never die!" He was right. My mother's rash act only increased my appetite for rock-n-roll. Thirty years later, I'm not only still listening to rock, I'm performing it in bars and clubs all over northern Michigan. I can play and sing more than 500 of rock's greatest hits by heart, and while I am certainly willing to concede that plenty of rock songs convey negative and even harmful messages, far more of them do precisely the opposite.

History has proven that the rock artists at Woodstock were closer to the truth about Vietnam than were the politicians in Washington. In the late 70s and early 80s, it was rock led projects like "USA for Africa" and "Artists Against Apartheid" that awakened America's conscience, along with my own, to famines, AIDS, and the rampant injustices our African brothers and sisters were enduring.

Rock's influence has never been more pervasive than it is in the new millennium, thanks to technologies like the i-pod and the mp3 player. Today's teens — and many adults — listen to hours of music a day and hundreds of songs each week. When the god-father of youth ministry, Tony Campolo, was asked what cultural forces he sees most influencing youth and young adults today, his response was immediate. "Music. I don't think we pay enough attention to music and the messages of the people who write it." While Campolo is ambivalent about whether music's overall influence is positive or negative, he is firm in his conclusion that, "music is clearly the dominant force for molding youth." (Youth Worker Magazine, May/June 06, p. 29) If Tony is right (and he usually is) then we ought to be listening to what rockers are saying.

I have been paying attention to and participating in rock-n-roll music for more than thirty years, and I've developed a profound respect for the deep spirituality of many rock songwriters and their so-called 'secular' music. In fact, rock-n-roll music has done two things to me that my mother never imagined: it has helped me tune into the often subtle voice of God, and it also influenced me to become a pastor.

Millions of good-hearted people of faith — and particularly Christians — continue to respond to rock music only with fear and anger. Some of the kids in my high school youth group have parents who react to their i-pod playlists the very same way my mom reacted to my record collection back in 1977. Christian publications continually warn parents of the corrupting filth in the rock culture. It seems some followers of

Christ aren't even aware that there are other, less fear-driven options for interacting with the 'secular' culture.

Rob Johnston's and Catherine Barsotti's book, *Finding God in the Movies,* offers a menu of options for responding to and interacting with popular culture. Their five-part typology is just as applicable to music as it is to film. Barsotti and Johnston believe that we can *avoid* secular contributions to the arts; be very *cautious* toward them; enter into a *dialogue* with them; *appropriate* their truths into our own; or we can see in secular art forms an opportunity for an *encounter with the divine.* (*Finding God in the Movies,* Barsotti & Johnston, Baker Books, pgs. 20–21) Most of the Christians I've been around in my lifetime really only respond to rock music with Barsotti and Johnston's first two options — avoidance or extreme caution. I, on the other hand, am far more interested in the other three options — entering a dialogue with rock music, appropriating its truths into my own, and even encountering God in it.

It has been through those final three options that I have come to hear the voice of God in popular, mainstream rock music. *The Gospel According to Rock* will develop and train your ears to hear God in a rock-n-roll lyric like, "Your prison is walking through this world all alone," or "You better let somebody love you before it's too late." (The Eagles, "Desperado")

As Mick Jagger once said, "I know, it's only rock-n-roll, but I like it." He who has ears to hear, let him hear.

Love of Neighbor

"The distant nation my community, the
street person my responsibility."
"Hammer & A Nail" – The Indigo Girls

I've been going to church my entire life, but I never knew what Apartheid was until I listened to U2's *Live at Red Rocks*. I couldn't find Ethiopia on a map, much less comprehend the extent of the famine there, until I heard Springsteen interviewed on MTV. It was Sting's single "They Dance Alone" that taught me about The Mothers of the Disappeared in Chile, and John Mellencamp and Neil Young opened my eyes to the plight of the small farmer here in the U.S. Yet so much of the media attention paid to rock throughout my lifetime has focused on its vulgar, profane, and sexually explicit lyrics. Do rock's critics even notice the social conscience, incredible generosity, and benevolence of the rock community? Rock musicians have collectively raised hundreds of millions of dollars to help small family farmers in America, AIDS victims on both American and African shores, famine victims throughout the world, and, more recently, victims of

9/11 and Hurricane Katrina. And on July 7, 2007, rock-n-rollers united 2 billion people from 7 continents to draw attention to the threat of global warming in their concert for the planet "Live Earth." Rock has been a powerful force for good, consistently helping those in need, even when many Christians and churches have not.

Rock's critics spend so much time and energy counting swear words, that they fail to notice the truly prophetic rock voices; the voices calling us to relieve human suffering wherever it rears its head. The first track on The Indigo Girls' early 90s release, *Nomads, Indians, & Saints*, "Hammer and a Nail," reminds us that "the distant nation (is) my community, the street person (is) my responsibility." Nearly two decades earlier, Supertramp, in their smash hit, "Give a Little Bit," called us to "see the man with the lonely eyes" and to "take his hand." The "give a little bit" message has been embraced by subsequent generations of rock fans as well, producing a huge hit for the Goo-Goo Dolls when they covered Supertramp's top-selling tune on one of their recent records. When Springsteen toured without The East Street Band to promote his *Ghost of Tom Joad* solo project, he told story after story of the downtrodden and oppressed, reminding audiences throughout the nation that it has always been our job to take care of the least of these. "Wherever there's a cop out beatin' a guy, wherever a hungry newborn baby cries...Look for me, mom, and I'll be there," says Springsteen, paraphrasing John Steinbeck. (Bruce Springsteen, "The Ghost of Tom Joad")

In 1978, The Doobie Brothers' monster hit, "Takin' It to the Streets," opened with "You don't know me but I'm your brother." In these eight words, Michael McDonald unveiled one of the most subtle and significant truths of our time: the pervasive and tragic separation between the haves and the have-nots in America. The rich and the poor don't even know each other any more, much less accept their God-given status as brothers. At times, it seems as if we've structured our cities, our suburbs, and even our churches in a way that rigidly separates groups along socio-economic lines. In communities like Harbor Springs, Michigan, where I live and work, kids can live the first 18 years of their lives without seeing a homeless person or ever having a face-to-face encounter with what McDonald calls, later in the song, "poverty's despair."

Shane Claiborne illustrates this sad truth of the unbridgeable distance between rich and poor in his book *The Irresistible Revolution*. He and his fellow revolutionaries were living in solidarity with some homeless folks in Philadelphia, who had moved into an abandoned cathedral. Claiborne's group received a package from a sympathetic, wealthy, suburban church marked: "For the homeless." "The entire box was filled with microwave popcorn." Claiborne laments, "We barely had electricity, much less a microwave, and popcorn wasn't on the top of the needs list…I wanted to cry because of how far the church had become removed from the poor." (Shane Claiborne, *The Irresistible Revolution*, Zondervan, 2006, p. 63)

Michael McDonald had it right when he sang, "You don't know my kind in your world." Just last Sunday in our upper-middle class, white church, a poor man came to our worship service to hear his daughter sing with our kids' choir. One of our kindest, most sensitive parishioners confessed later that, "I saw this guy and could tell by his clothes that he was poor and not a regular here. I really wanted to welcome him and treat him like everyone else, but as I walked up to him, I just froze up. I didn't know what to say."

"Takin' it to the Streets," and the countless other rock songs with similar themes, should serve as reminders to all of us. Regardless of socio-economic class or religious background, we are brothers and sisters. Marvin Gaye understood the inherent connectedness of all human beings in his 1971 mega-hit, "What's Going On?" He began with "Brother, Brother, there's too many people dying." Marvin knew that war was "not the answer," and that we should apply ourselves to bringing "some loving here today." Rock-n-rollers from Motown all the way to L.A. have known for decades that with our God-ordained, familial bond come moral obligations. Avoiding the poor or structuring our lives so as not to notice the poverty all around us does not relieve us of the responsibility God has placed upon us to care for "the least of these, our brothers and sisters." (Matthew 25:40) Those who claim to follow Christ, Yahweh, and even Allah are called on and expected to provide for the poor and disenfranchised.

In the last 50 years, it has been the rock-n-roll world that has given us prophets to further the tradition of Old Testament figures like Isaiah, voicing concern that God's children were, "turning away from our own flesh and blood." (Isaiah 58:7) Callous humans throughout history have tried to ignore their poor brothers and sisters, often justifying their apathy with the words of Christ himself in Matthew 26:11: "The poor will always be with you." Thankfully, rock-n-rollers have exposed this heinous and heartless misinterpretation for what it is — more Ayn Rand-ian than Christian.

Those of us both in and out of the church are indebted to the rock artists, who, like the prophets of old, have reminded us of our sacred and moral obligation to our poor brothers and sisters, our siblings in the great human family. We are connected. As the Apostle Paul writes in I Corinthians 12, "You are the body of Christ, and each of you is a part of it…If one part suffers, every other part suffers with it." (I Corinthians 12:27, 26) There are those both in and outside the rock community who believe that we can and should end hunger and extreme poverty in our lifetime. An ambitious goal, indeed, but the outspoken lead singer of U2, Bono, is leading the charge, insisting that it can be done. He and other rockers are dedicating their lives and huge portions of their income to eradicating poverty and hunger.

In February 2006, it was Bono who was selected by President Bush to speak at the National Prayer Breakfast. In his self-deprecating opening remarks, Bono acknowledged how odd it was for a rock-n-roller to be addressing such an august gathering of world leaders and political power brokers. But he went on to say that,

> "Africa makes a fool of our idea of justice; it makes a farce of our idea of equality. It mocks our pieties, it doubts our concerns, it questions our commitment. 6,500 Africans are still dying every day from preventable, treatable disease, for lack of drugs we can buy at any drug store…there's no way we can look at what's happening in Africa and, if we're honest, conclude that deep down, we really accept

that Africans are equal to us. Anywhere else in the world, we wouldn't accept it. Look at what happened in South East Asia with the Tsunami. 150,000 lives lost…In Africa, 150,000 lives are lost every month…God will not accept that. Mine won't at least. Will yours?"

(www.data.org/archives/000774.php)

Followers of Christ have no choice but to care for what Jesus called "the least of these" in our society. (Matthew 25:40) More than half of Jesus' parables focus on treatment of the poor and the disenfranchised. His very first public words, as he began his ministry, came from the prophet Isaiah, proclaiming "good news to the poor." (Isaiah 61:1-2, Luke 4:18-19) Unfortunately, most churches and Christian communities have tended to spend far more time, energy, and money taking care of themselves and their buildings than they have spent taking care of others. Thankfully, rock bands have called us back to Christ's essential mission. It is high time we listened to them.

Freedom

"Freedom — that's just some people talkin'
Your prison is walkin' through this world all alone."
"Desperado" – The Eagles

It seems like my whole life has been spent thinking that freedom was around the next corner. When I was on my trike, I was sure that freedom would be found on two wheels. Not much later, when my older brothers started driving, I realized what a difference two more wheels and an engine could make in my pursuit of freedom. Next, it was the thought of going away to college that epitomized true freedom. And yet, as a college student, I fantasized about how free I would be when I no longer had so much school work and studying to do. Even now, at 45, I'm still looking around that next corner, thinking retirement must be the sweetest freedom of all.

From rock's very beginning, freedom has been at the core of its value system. As Steve Turner notes in *The Gospel According to The Beatles*, for rock-n-rollers like the Fab Four, "the human problem…was one of limitations and constraint. We couldn't reach our full potential if we were inhibited." (Turner, *The Gospel According to The Beatles*, Westminster John Knox, 2006, p. 8) In other words, as far as rock-n-roll is concerned, human rules, constraints, and conventions are the problem, and freedom from them is the answer. And so in "Revolution" John Lennon and The Beatles sang, "one thing I can tell you is you got to be free." Crosby, Stills, Nash, & Young not only found the "cost of freedom," but also bashed President Nixon and the Ohio National Guard for gunning down legitimate expressions of freedom in "Ohio." Meanwhile, Bob Dylan was asking that same generation how it felt, "to be on your own, with no direction home, like a rolling stone." Once we add Springsteen's "Born to Run," Lou Reed's "Take a Walk on the Wild Side," Steppenwolf's "Magic Carpet Ride," and countless others to the list, it would be tempting for us to conclude that rock's definition of freedom — throwing off all restraint — is purely hedonistic and utterly incompatible with Christian teachings on the matter.

When we add the so-called "rock-n-roll lifestyle" to the discussion, the chasm separating rock's understanding of freedom from Christianity's grows both deeper and wider. Think of Elvis's pelvic gyrations, Jim Morrison exposing himself on stage, David Bowie performing in drag, and the "long, strange trip" the Grateful Dead and their Dead-heads took. What was Woodstock, if not a massive celebration of a no-rules variety of freedom? The concert itself, on Yasgur's farm, charged no admission price. Kids and adults alike stripped naked, danced in the mud, and were free to do whatever they wanted. Beatles' biographer Steve Turner was right on when he wrote that rockers used "their attitude; how they dressed, the way they behaved, the energy they created on stage, and what they said during interviews," to express themselves. (Turner, p. 78) While Turner wrote this specifically of The Beatles, clearly it applies to rockers in general, as does his conclusion. "Everything about them, from their style of hair to their surrealistic answers to journalists' questions, implied that boundaries were to be challenged and that personal freedom began with being true to oneself." (Turner, p. 78)

We must dig deeper into the canon of rock-n-roll lyrics if we want a more thorough understanding of freedom than the one we find floating on rock's surface. While rock-n-roll has and will always have its advocates of an individualistic, hedonistic, no-rules variety of freedom, its wisest and most mature voices understand that true freedom cannot be found through long hair, mountains of pills, and all the groupies rock stardom can buy.

In "Redemption Song," Bob Marley called his listeners to "emancipate" themselves "from mental slavery." His was a freedom of mind, imagination, and spirit. Steve Turner noted that as The Beatles matured,

> "the issues that preoccupied them changed from seeking freedom from authority and tradition to searching for freedom from material craving, rampant ego…You could rattle human authority by growing your hair long, but you couldn't conquer your inner demons in the same way. To 'change your head,' as John (Lennon) referred to it in "Revolution," required something much more radical."
> (Turner, p. 8)

The Eagles, once accused of being Satanists when *Hotel California* was released, offered a profoundly spiritual take on freedom in "Desperado." Don Henley pleads with his listener, who may think he is free but is actually in a prison. The desperado's problem is not that he is constrained or limited by societal conventions. His problem is that there is nothing or no one to which he is committed. Even though "some fine things" have come his way, the pitiful desperado "only wants the ones that" he "can't get." The message of this brilliant, top-selling song from 1973 is that while the desperado lives under the illusion of freedom, he is, in fact, far from it. The desperado's deepest need, though he does not even recognize it, is for love, genuine, committed love. Henley ends the song calling the desperado to "let somebody love you before it's too late."

Here we begin to see where rock-n-roll and the Christian gospel are far more similar than we first expected. When Jesus uttered the counter-intuitive truth that "If anyone seeks to save his own life, he will lose it; but whoever loses his life for my sake will surely find it," could he have been suggesting that a life lived in hedonistic freedom from all restraint is far less satisfying than one lived in committed service to others? (Matthew 16:25)

The freedom Jesus spoke of was one that could not only co-exist with commitment, but could actually thrive within it. For Jesus, the most important freedom — Freedom with a capital F — comes from knowing the Truth, with a capital T. "If you hold to my teaching," Jesus said, "you are really my disciples. Then you will know the truth and the truth will set you free." (John 8:31-32) The freedom Christ spoke of, lived, and offered to his followers was not incompatible with commitment, nor was it available only in heaven or in some utopian afterlife. As Harvard Chaplain, Peter Gomes, notes, freedom to Jesus was a freedom FOR rather than a freedom FROM. Jesus actually believed that those who committed themselves to following Him would experience the most comprehensive and fulfilling freedom of all. (Peter Gomes, *Strength for the Journey*, p. 23)

"Freedom FOR what?" we might ask. What exactly does a commitment to Christ free one for? The freedom I've experienced in Christ has encouraged me to be myself and to be true to who I am. After all, if God created me uniquely, with all my gifts and all my warts, why should I ever seek to be anyone other than myself? Freedom in Christ has also allowed me to let go of a growing percentage of my annual income, so that it might be used to meet more pressing needs than any my family and I will ever experience. The freedom Christ offers has freed me to live both more passionately and compassionately, without fearing what I might lose as I offer myself in service to others. The Christian path has also freed me for genuine and respectful interaction with my brothers and sisters from other religions, knowing that the God to whom I am committed is far bigger than any human, religious construct, including the one I call my own.

Those who view rock's understanding of freedom as utterly incompatible with Christianity have misunderstood both rock and Christianity. Too many people have mistakenly come to associate the Christian path with the absence of freedom, as if becoming a Christian is tantamount to putting on a straight jacket that permanently and irrevocably limits the human experience, heaping upon it a list of puritanical "thou shalt not's." When Jesus said, "The kingdom of God is within you," I think he meant it. When he said "In knowing me, you will know the truth and the truth will set you free," Jesus wasn't talking about a "Born to run," "roll-me-away"-from-all-commitments freedom. Jesus meant that when we truly connect with our Creator and offer ourselves completely to the building of something much bigger than ourselves — something Jesus called "the kingdom of God" — we will be free in ways that make hedonistic pleasure seeking seem not only selfish but small-minded. I like the way mega-church mogul Rob Bell defines freedom in his latest work, *Sex God:* "Freedom isn't being able to have whatever we crave. Freedom is going without whatever we crave and being fine with it." (Rob Bell, *Sex God,* Zondervan, 2007, p. 75)

Many of rock's elder statesmen have come to understand, often at great cost to themselves, that pursuing the kind of no restraints freedom that they, themselves, once championed, has its cost. Sex, drugs, and rock stardom may sound and seem wonderful at first, but Elvis, Jimi Hendrix, Janis Joplin, Kurt Cobain, and countless other rock heroes are a constant reminder of where that kind of hedonistic lifestyle inevitably leads. The rockers who live long enough come to understand that such hedonistic pursuits are far more apt to turn one into a slave than to set him free. Eugene Peterson puts it this way in his paraphrased translation of the Bible.

> *"You know well enough from your own experience that there are some acts of so-called freedom that destroy freedom. Offer yourselves to sin, for instance, and it's your last free act. But offer yourselves to the ways of God and the freedom never quits."*
> (Eugene Peterson, *The Message,* Romans 6:15-17)

American Poet, James Kavanaugh, writes powerfully of the price so many have paid in pursuing a freedom that is incompatible with any sort of commitment.

> *"Loneliness has taken its toll as I feared
> that I might miss some freedom
> in my commitment to you."*
> (James Kavanaugh, "Of Loneliness," From Loneliness to Love,
> Harper & Row, 1986, p. 59)
> used with permission.

Kavanaugh, like so many free-wheeling artists and rockers, was seduced into thinking that forsaking all others would cost him too much freedom. It was, as the Eagles suggested it would be, "too late" when Kavanaugh figured out that the ultimate freedom is to be found within the context of commitment rather than outside of it.

If we listen to what the more mature rock artists are saying about freedom, another, more spiritual definition of it emerges, one that is surprisingly consistent with the teachings of Jesus. Genuine freedom entails self-sacrifice rather than self-seeking. Freedom is more about losing one's self in commitment to others than committing only to self. "For whoever seeks to save his own life will lose it, but whoever loses his life for my sake and the gospel will surely find it." (Matthew 16:25)

Identity

"Can you see the real me? Can you?
"The Real Me" – The Who

At the very epicenter of human spirituality is the question "Who am I?" Socrates' oft' quoted admonition to "know thyself," coupled with the universal human yearning to discover one's purpose in life, are central concerns in civilized societies. It is our interest in identity and purpose that has fueled and funded the multi-billion dollar self-help industry and has put Rick Warren on the map as the author of the best selling non-fiction work of all time, *The Purpose-driven Life*. Americans today spend an inordinate amount of our time, energy, and money trying to work out our identities and clarify our sense of how we fit into the larger world.

Rock-n-roll is equally interested in such questions of identity. Check out Bob Dylan's "What Good Am I?" Steve Miller's "The Joker," Alice Cooper's "I'm Eighteen," or Edie Brickell's "What I Am," and you'll get a quick sense of how much rock-n-roll energy has gone into the "who am I?" question.

In their gut-wrenchingly raw 1973 anthem, "The Real Me," The Who articulated the universal spiritual yearning to be known, understood, and accepted. Which of us hasn't wanted to scream at some point, "Can you see the real me?" to some or even all of the folks who matter most to us? The Who's notion of a "real me" stands in stark contrast to the "Substitute" of which they sang just a few years earlier. In that 1966 release, the young "Who-ligans" saw right through the props that they, themselves, had used to project a false image to the world. "I look pretty tall but my heels are high…my fine looking suit is really made out of sack." Then, in 1978, they took up the identity question a third time in an even more direct fashion in "Who are you?" This five-minute exercise in creative redundancy repeats the "who are you" question more times than I was able to count.

But rock's interest in identity goes much further than one question and one band. Rockers have also sought to tackle the equally complicated question of our purpose as humans. Bob Dylan wondered "What good am I…if I turn my back as you silently die?" (Bob Dylan, "What Good Am I?") The Beatles sang derisively of what it was like to go through life without a sense of self and without a purpose in their 60s hit "Nowhere Man." "Doesn't have a point of view, knows not where he's going to." Much of my time as a youth pastor is spent with teenagers who are struggling mightily to forge their own identities and to carve out an understanding of their purpose in life, amidst all manner of confusion and mixed messages.

The Judeo-Christian tradition puts significant emphasis on identity in both the Old and New Testaments. Many theologians correctly point to Genesis 1:27 as the central biblical basis for our identity as humans. We are made in the image of God. So, too, is everyone else, regardless of race, nationality, religion or any other human category. Earth, Wind, and Fire put it this way: "You're a shining star, no matter who you are! Shining bright to see what you can truly be." (Earth, Wind, & Fire, "Shining Star") It is coming to know and own this truth — our image of God status — that liberates each of us to be that "shining star," that God made us to be.

Harvard Chaplain Peter Gomes tells the story of a visit Nelson Mandela made to Harvard University.

> "What distinguished Nelson Mandela and allowed him to stand above and beyond so many of us…is the very simple, unsophisticated fact that this is a man who knows who he is. This is a man whose ideals are intact…He has been neither seduced nor intimidated by what others think; rather, his authority — gravitas combined with grace — comes from that sense of knowing who he is and from being secure, stable in his sense of worth and being."
>
> (Peter Gomes, "Who do you think you are?" in *Strength for the Journey*, Harper Collins, 2004, p. 82)

Brennan Manning calls this self-knowledge and sense of self-worth the "beautiful transparency" of "honest disciples who never wear a false face and do not pretend to be anything but who they are." (Manning, *The Ragamuffin Gospel*, Multnomah Publishers, Inc., 1990, p. 85)

I wish I could claim to have been Mandela-like in my own quest for identity. But the truth is I was well into my 30s before I had a clue as to who I was. I even got into the ministry some twenty years ago for all the wrong reasons and was neither beautiful nor transparent in my discipleship. Not only did I not know who I was, I had even less of an idea what I was doing leading a 250 member church! After three unsustainable years, I took what turned out to be a thirteen-year hiatus from parish ministry, one that included everything from psychotherapy to contemplative prayer and from self-denial to hedonism, before discovering who I was and what God had made me to do.

Part of my slowness in coming to terms with my identity was caused by the false assumption that I needed to hide or cover up those parts of me of which I was ashamed. I didn't know how or where my own negative baggage fit into the real me, much less into God's purpose for my life. My weaknesses and human failings were and are real, regrettable, and even embarrassing: my alcohol tainted family system and the scars I carry from it; my failure at marriage and the baggage that comes with that; and my on-going battle with lust and sexual fantasy. Understandably, I've tried to conceal these less attractive parts of who I am and have even pretended that they aren't a part of my genuine self. Not owning up to these deeper truths of my identity has kept me from experiencing that "beautiful transparency" Brennan Manning spoke of and the freeing joy that comes from living authentically.

It was actually an amazing dream I had in my mid 30s that helped me move to a new and beautiful phase in my search for identity. I dreamt that I was at the "pearly gates," though I remember no pearl nor any gates. There was just a cloudy haze all around me, and I was awaiting my turn to see G-O-D. I was pacing restlessly in my dream, obsessing over all of my regrettable sins. A slideshow of shame was playing in my head as I paced. It was a greatest hits highlight reel of all my sins. As each sin flashed on the big HD screen in my mind, I would think, "Is this the one God is going to confront me with first?" I was sweating and stressed beyond measure. (I would later awaken with my sheets and pillow completely soaked.) Then The Voice came, calling my name — "TOBY…" I stopped breathing…The next word introduced a question…"WHY…" and was followed by the longest, most uncomfortable pause I've ever endured. During this eternity of God's silence, I started finishing — in my head — the question I was sure God was about to ask me… "WHY…did you treat the alcoholics in your life with so much judgment and so little compassion?" "WHY…did you break up with and bail out on your college sweetheart, who moved across the country to be with you — at your request — within a few weeks of her relocating?" "WHY…did you spend so much energy trying to get your step kids to keep the house clean and so little energy just playing with them and enjoying their company?" "Why…did you do so little to relieve the suffering all around you?"

Suddenly, my speculative questions gave way to The Voice. He repeated the "WHY" but this time finished the question … "Why did you fail to be yourself?" "Why did you fail to be yourself?" *This* was the question God had for me? *This* was His primary gripe about the life I lived? No mention of particular sins or of the many people I'd hurt over the years, just "Why did you fail to be yourself?"

I don't know how long it was after awaking from that dream that I realized that this was and still is the ultimate question, not only for me, but for all of us: "Why did you fail to be yourself?" If we're serious about our belief in a God who created us individually and uniquely, and who fashioned each of us, not only with a purpose — something unique to offer the world — but with the tools and traits to fulfill that purpose, wouldn't it be a slap in God's face for any of us to attempt to be anyone other than ourselves?

That dream deepened my commitment to the real me and to living authentically out of that real me self. As Bono said so eloquently,

> "I used to think that one day I'd be able to resolve the different drives I have in different directions, the tension between the different people I am. Now I realize that is who I am, and I'm more content to be discontent."
> (*U2 by U2*, Harper Collins, 2006, p. 345)

As I have gradually come to terms with the less attractive and often contradictory parts of who I am, and as I've let others in on those darker aspects of my identity, I've found grace and understanding where I least expected it and have discovered a healing power in my ministry that has deepened my understanding of how and why Christ used his "wounds" to heal us. (Isaiah 53:5) My shameful past and sinful present keep me real. They root out my tendency to judge others. I'm not sure what Paul's "thorn in the flesh" was (see II Cor 12:7-10), but I'm fairly certain that God didn't take it away because it was a central part of Paul's self, a part that, like every other part of Paul, God could use, not only to bring Paul closer to God, but to bring others closer to their Creator through Paul.

I will never be proud of the shameful regrets I carry, the less attractive parts of my identity. A huge part of me still wishes that they'd never happened and that they could just be stricken from the record — mine, God's, and the world's. In Christ, however, I can't help but recognize that my greatest points of shame are largely responsible for the grace, mercy, and tolerance that have become the hallmarks of my life and ministry. I spend a lot of time caring for those going through divorce and for those dealing with an alcoholic family member. My ministry with men who are fighting what Arterburn & Stoeker call "every man's struggle," otherwise known as lust, never seems to slow down. (*every man's battle*, Waterbrook Press, 2000)

I'm back in the parish ministry, and what has made all the difference this time around is that "I know what I am, if you know what I mean."(Edie Brickell, "What I Am") This time around I serve God and His church out of a radical and uncompromising commitment to the real me. I am a child of God, "a shining star." All the scars, sins, and wounds in the world can't change the fact that I am a child of God, created in His beautiful image. It took me far too long to come to the realization that God didn't need to turn me into someone else or remove the blemishes of my past in order for me to function effectively and fully in ministry. In *The Ragamuffin Gospel*, Brennan Manning puts it this way: "Getting honest with ourselves does not make us unacceptable to God. It does not distance us from God, but draws us to Him — as nothing else can — and opens us anew to the flow of grace." (*The Ragamuffin Gospel*, Multnomah Publishers, 1990, p. 85)

The hit rock trio of the 70s, America, had it right when they sang: "Oz never did give nothing to the Tin Man that he didn't already have." (America, "Tin Man") Each of us already has what we need to be faithful, compassionate followers of God. Each of has the unmistakable, irremovable mark of our Creator upon us and within us, the image of God. Each of us bears wounds that, like the wounds of Christ, can heal others, if only we will expose and own up to them. Rock music from the last five decades has helped me get in touch with my wounds, my true self, the Real Me. Rock lyrics have helped me come to see myself as gifted and to see my sins and particular burdens as a part of that giftedness.

I am a child of God. I always have had and always will have a sliver of the Divine within me. Knowing and resting in that has made all the difference.

Loneliness

"Seems I'm not alone in being alone.
A hundred billion castaways looking for a home."
"Message in a Bottle" – The Police

If you've never had the experience of being completely alone in the middle of 2,500 people — many of whom are your own schoolmates — count your blessings. For me, it was a weekly occurrence in the mid 1970s. My brother, two years older than I, was a starter on the Bay High Varsity football squad. I wasn't. In fact, I was forbidden even to try out for football by my well-intentioned, overly cautious parents, who saw me as a midget-sized accident waiting to happen. I was, however, deemed fit enough to attend my brother's games under the Friday night lights. The problem was that I had no one with whom to go to the games. So I'd go by myself. About the only place worse to be alone at age 15 is the school cafeteria, where, Monday through Friday, from 11:34 to 12:14, I'd sit at the same table in the far corner under the clock, by myself, eating the brown-bagged lunch I'd made to spare myself the additional humiliation of having to stand in the lunch line with no one to talk to.

19

Thirty-some years later, in my work as a pastor, I interact with at least one person every day who is dealing with what Sting and The Police call, "more loneliness than any man can bear." (The Police, "Message in a Bottle") A few days ago, it was a 75-year-old widow who can't seem to adjust to life without her husband. Last week it was a high school sophomore, who hasn't been able to find a home in any of the tightly defined cliques at Harbor High. He's taken to cutting himself in attempt to feel connected to something, if only his own pain. This morning it was a woman in her late 40s who tried to take her own life a few weeks ago. As she poured out her story to me, loneliness and despair covered her like a heavy, wet blanket. Her husband had left her for another woman. Her kids are out of the nest and busy with their own lives. She has become so negative and draining to be with that the few friends she once had don't come around anymore.

During my lean and lonely adolescent years, I did what I've done so often throughout my life: I sought refuge in my basement, surrounded by vinyl records and 8-track tapes. I remember singing along with America, "This is for all the lonely people, thinking their lives have passed them by." (America, "Lonely People") I remember trying to figure out if Simon and Garfunkel were being serious or sarcastic when they sang, "I am a rock. I am an island." (Simon and Garfunkel, "I Am a Rock") But the one that always got me most was James Taylor's "Fire and Rain." "I've seen lonely times when I could not find a friend." I don't know how many times I've sung along with that one. Back in 1975, there was all kinds of speculation about that song and whether James was in the Funny Farm when he wrote it, who Suzanne was, and whether she really killed herself or died in a plane crash. All that mattered to me, however, was that J.T. was a guy who knew what it felt like to be lonely. I needed that.

My oldest brother's Beatles' albums were a forbidden treasure I'd listen to only when absolutely certain he was out of the house and not likely to return. I remember discovering "Eleanor Rigby" and feeling like we could be friends if I could ever locate her church. "Ah, look at all the lonely people!" The tightly drawn, pitiable characters of Father MacKenzie and Miss Rigby in an empty church, picking up rice after a wedding, and ultimately being "buried along with her name;" these were people with whom I felt an instant kinship.

Had my loneliness endured into the 80s, I know my spirit would have been lifted by The Police's "Message in a Bottle." That song may be the most profound treatment of loneliness I've ever heard. Its opening image is of "a castaway lost at sea." Sting's lonesome loser puts a message in a bottle, casts it out upon the waters, and hopes against hope that somebody out there — anybody — will receive and respond to his S.O.S. An entire year passes with no response, drowning whatever prospect the castaway had for a rescue (or at least a pen pal). He chastises himself for not knowing "right from the start" that his efforts to ease his loneliness were futile.

The Hebrew scriptures speak of loneliness as a symptom of our brokenness as humans. Psalm 22 voices the Psalmist's complaint that, "I am a worm and not a man, scorned by men and despised by the people. All who see me mock me; they hurl insults, shaking their heads." The twenty-fifth Psalm says, "Turn to me and be gracious to me, for I am lonely and afflicted," while the thirty-first adds, "I am the utter contempt of my neighbors; I am a dread to my friends — those who see me on the street flee from me. I am forgotten by them as though I were dead; I have become like broken pottery." Old Testament loneliness includes a sense of being forgotten even by God: "My God, my God, why have you forsaken me?" (Psalm 22)

Twentieth century American Poet, James Kavanaugh, calls loneliness "the painful, relentless destroyer of human life." He goes on to say that loneliness "is not reserved for the aged, but can strike the young and middle-aged as well." To Kavanaugh, the only "antidote to loneliness is love." (*From Loneliness to Love,* Harper & Row, 1986, p. 1) used with permission.

The New Testament's treatment of loneliness is equally thorough and profound. Jesus seemed to have a special compassion for the lonely wherever he went. He stopped to listen to and to heal Bartimaeus, the blind beggar; he singled out Zacchaeus, the least popular guy in all of Jericho, had dinner with and stayed with him; Jesus even spoke with and served a man who had been lying all alone by the pool of

Bethsaida for 38 years. But in John 4, Jesus has his most stunning exchange with a woman who may well be the loneliest woman in all of scripture. She is an unnamed Samaritan, a member of that scorned, half-breed tribe that Jews were taught to hate. This particular woman's loneliness was, no doubt, intensified by the fact that she had been married five times, making her an untouchable, even among her own people. It explains her seemingly idiotic choice of coming to get water from the town well at noon. Not only would that have been the hottest time of the day to lug a heavy bucket of water several miles, but carrying the water in the heat of the day would also have guaranteed that a significant portion of the water would evaporate long before she ever got it home. Most Biblical scholars conclude that the only reason anyone would have chosen to head to the well at high noon was to avoid any and all contact with other people. This Samaritan woman was a social castaway, doomed to live a life where each sunrise brought another lonely day, with no one with whom to talk.

Jesus' encounter with this lonely Samaritan is stunning in every respect. First, Jews, like Jesus, were not even supposed to acknowledge Samaritans, much less converse with them. Jews would literally walk all the way around Samaria just to avoid setting foot inside its defiled borders. On top of that, Jewish men were not to speak to women in public, much less sit and talk with them at length, the way Jesus did in John 4. This is why his disciples "were surprised to find him talking with a woman." But most stunning of all, in John's fourth chapter, is the fact that Jesus does not mock, deride, nor condemn this horribly lonely woman for her past, not even for her marital history. Instead, Jesus makes it clear that although he knows all about her life, he will neither mistreat her nor ostracize her because of it. Instead, the Nazarene sits with her, engaging her in a conversation that must have been the first and longest talk she'd had in years. Jesus knew that this Samaritan woman was "so tired of being alone." (John Mayer, "Love Song for No One") Jesus soothes her loneliness with his indiscriminate, extravagant love.

For Sting and The Police, there is no cure for loneliness in "Message in a Bottle." There is, however, a salve that soothes it. It comes in the form of "a hundred billion bottles" that have arrived at the castaway's shore. The one bottle that the lone castaway set out to sea, carrying a single S.O.S. note, elicited a hundred billion responses. "Seems I'm not alone in being alone" the lonely man concludes.

There is no joyful reunion with a lover at the song's end. There is no rescue boat that shows up. There is only the assurance that the lonely castaway is "not alone in being alone." The hope in "Message in a Bottle" comes from the universal loneliness that we all share, our common feeling of not belonging, of not being connected. The "hundred billion bottles" aren't exactly what the castaway had hoped for, but they are, it seems, enough.

Keeping the Sabbath

"You thought you would be satisfied, but
you never will — learn to be still."
"Learn to Be Still" – The Eagles

I was racing home from a hectic day at work,
bearing down on the annoying slowpoke in front of me, when I heard
Don Henley's "In a New York Minute" for the first time. I pulled off
to the side of the road in stunned silence, feeling as if Henley — or
perhaps Someone even bigger than he — had been singing directly
to me. The song opens with the all-too-brief story of Harry, who one
morning went down to the train station and never came back. His
black clothes were later discovered scattered across the railroad tracks,
and the verse concludes starkly with "and he won't be down on Wall
Street in the morning." The song's title is also its repeated refrain —
"In a New York minute everything can change."

Everything CAN change in a New York minute, an Oklahoma City
minute, a Lancaster, Pennsylvania minute, or even in a Virginia Tech
minute. One person's 'everything' can change in a single moment in a

doctor's office when test results arrive, in a fraction of a second when an on-coming car suddenly crosses the median, or on an elementary school playground when that tiny, five year-old hand loses its grip on the highest monkey bar.

Though most of us know the deep-down truth that "everything can change in a New York minute," such knowledge still isn't quite enough to really slow us down, at least not for long. We Americans live at break-neck speed, packing more into a single day than many of our ancestors attempted in a week. The kids in my high school youth group have schedules that make my head spin. Up at the crack of dawn, they're rushed to school, where every moment is scheduled. Immediately after school, they're picked up and rushed to their sports practice or their music lesson — sometimes both! No time for dinner at home, not with an SAT prep class starting at 6:30 p.m., then it's back to school for an evening play practice. Finally arriving home at 9:30 p.m., thoroughly exhausted, they're just in time to get started on two to three hours of homework. We've taught them pretty well, haven't we?

As a long-time follower of Christ and a professional pastor, I probably should have figured out by now how to live at a more reasonable pace. I'm pretty good at quoting James Taylor's, "the secret of life is enjoying the passage of time," (James Taylor, "The Secret of Life") and I know all the words to Simon & Garfunkel's 59th St. Bridge Song: "Slow down, you move to fast." Yet I don't live in light of their deep truths.

There's another Eagles' song that has hurried my attempt to slow down. It's called "Learn to Be Still." It came out a long time ago, but I must have been too busy to listen to it. In this tune, Don Henley sings of not being able to "silence" all the voices in his mind. He calls us "sheep without a shepherd," (where have I heard that line before…?) not knowing "how to be alone," when all we really need to do, Henley concludes, is "learn to be still."

It's a great and profound song, but I bet even The Eagles would admit that urging others to slow down is not a particularly original idea. Jews and Christians were supposed to have been doing it for somewhere in the neighborhood of 4,000 years. Yahweh, in His wisdom, anticipated our tendency to live life in the fast lane and gave us a commandment (not a suggestion): to spend one day in every seven slowing down and being still. The fourth commandment is to "remember the Sabbath and keep it holy." (Exodus 20:8-11) Jews and Christians have always been called to keep the Sabbath once a week. And, yet, what do most of us do with our Sabbath, our divinely provided day of rest? Lawn chores, gardening, running errands, shuttling our kids to Sunday sports practices, and getting a head start on the busy week to come. It hardly seems to be what our Maker had in mind when He gave us the most gracious commandment of all. And it really is a commandment of grace. The command to keep Sabbath is not supposed to fall heavily upon us, like one more thing we must do in order to keep God happy. Quite the opposite, the Sabbath command to slow down one day out of every seven is God's best attempt to keep us — his precious, beloved children — happy and healthy, balanced and sane, free from depression and hyper-stress, and as far from manic episodes and suicidal tendencies as He possibly can. Most of all, the Sabbath is God's attempt to remind us that it's not what we DO that makes God love us. It's not what we produce that brings our Heavenly Father pleasure. It is simply who we are. We are God's. It is He who has made us and called us His own, and it's only in slowing down and being still that we can ever come to know and to trust that.

Everything can change in a New York minute, in a heartbeat, and our spiritual response to that undeniable reality should be to slow down, to recognize and discern what is truly important. There are so many things we miss when we live life too quickly, without ever being still. David Lynch's brilliant 1999 film "The Straight Story" is arguably the slowest moving film of all time. It focuses on a 73-year-old man driving from Laurens, Iowa to Mt. Zion, Wisconsin…in a John Deer lawn tractor…at five miles an hour…towing a trailer that makes the Beverly Hillbillies look posh by comparison. But the power and profundity of Lynch's inordinately slow film is how much we, along with Alvin Straight, are able to notice at that speed. Not only is the slow driving, slow living Alvin Straight a grounded man of peace, but the troubled folks he encounters on his odyssey are lifted up and set free by their slow-paced encounters with him.

Youth pastor and writer Mark Yaconelli learned something of Alvin Straight's secret from his pregnant wife. Yaconelli writes,

> "When my wife was pregnant with our first child, she noticed that she rarely felt the baby move when she was actively running errands and doing chores around the house. Only when she stopped, sat still, or lay down could she feel the baby's activity. Sometimes at night, I would have my own private moments with our unborn child. I would wait until Jill fell asleep, then I would reach over and place my hand on her stomach. I would lie there feeling the baby shifting and moving. I would sit in wonder at this growing person, stirring inside. Noticing God requires the same attentiveness. Unless we regularly stop our activity and sit still for a moment…we miss God's Spirit moving within and around us."
>
> (Yaconelli, *Contemplative Youth Ministry*,
> Youth Specialties, 2006, p. 74)

Sabbath stillness is designed to help us be more observant and appreciative of what God is doing all around us. Yet, there is even more wisdom and buried treasure hidden in the fourth commandment. It's no accident that the holiest, purest guides and seekers in every religion are those who have learned to be still. The Dahli Lama, Mahatma Gandhi, Thomas Merton, the Buddha, and Jesus of Nazareth — ALL of them — spent time each and every day emptying themselves and seeking total internal silence and stillness. All of the great spiritual pioneers regularly put themselves in a position of receptivity, where they could listen to their Creator, the One who knows our every need.

Learning to be still in God's presence is hard. It's a spiritual discipline that few, if any, seem to master. Even those of us who are pastors and should know better get way too caught up in doing — visiting parishioners, counseling, teaching, running workshops, planning youth gatherings, equipping people for ministry, leading worship, writing and preaching sermons. How tempting it becomes, in all that doing, to measure the depth of our faith, our connection to God, by the hours we spend scrambling on the job. I have long struggled to celebrate the Sabbath, even when I'm on vacation! So I immediately start looking for a project, something I can DO. It often takes me the first three or four days just to get used to the fact that I don't have to be doing anything. Stillness makes me antsy and, my wife would add, not particularly pleasant. It's as if I am incapable of simply being content with what is right here in front of me, namely my wife, my children, and my God.

So I remind my parishioners all the time that if they want to pray for me, they can just use the words from a couple of Eagles' songs. "Lord, help Toby learn to be still. Help him remember that everything can change in a New York Minute." They can even throw in the famous first line from Simon and Garfunkel's "59th Street Bridge Song" if they'd like: "Lord, help Toby 'slow down, he moves too fast.'"

Psalm 46 tells us, "God is our refuge and our strength, an ever-present help in times of trouble. Therefore, we should not fear, though the earth give way and the mountains fall into the sea...for the Lord almighty IS with us." (Psalm 46:1-3, 7) And the Psalmist concludes that what we most need to do in our lives is, "Be still and know that I am God." (Psalm 46:10)

Will we ever learn? Will we ever learn to be still and receive the grace hidden in the Sabbath command? The Eagles don't seem to think so, for they end "Learn to Be Still" repeating, "You just keep on runnin'...You just keep on runnin.'"

For me, paying careful attention to rock-n-roll lyrics like that is what slows me down and rekindles my interest in and appreciation of the Sabbath and of what God was after in commanding us to keep it. Who would have thought that the spiritual profundity of several rock songs would lead me back into the Bible with a hunger to reconnect with God's most gracious commandment? With God, all things are possible, and all channels are useful.

Faith, Politics, and Prophets

*"Both sides... killing in God's name, but God
is nowhere to be found conveniently."*
"Marker in the Sand" – Pearl Jam

American history, for its non-indigenous people, began with a group of Europeans who risked everything to obtain religious freedom. It was a freedom to practice and live out their faith, whatever faith that might be. How ironic that 230 years later, that same nation — initially built on the idea of religious freedom — has become hell-bent on religious conformity within its borders and the assertion of Christian supremacy without.

In Old Testament times, the people of Israel became similarly puffed up, religiously arrogant, and too blind to notice their own hypocrisy. It was in such times that God sent a prophet — someone from outside the religious and political power structure — who would call Israel back to its covenant with Yahweh. That covenant emphasized that no matter how zealously they worshiped God, the Israelites needed to be caring for the poor, the disenfranchised, and the widows in order for their worship to be acceptable to Yahweh.

31

America in the 21st century may be in need of just such a prophetic wake-up call. Our religious arrogance and hypocrisy may be
catching up with us. An odd-looking, leather-clad, tattooed, body-
pierced, locust-eating, modern-day prophet might be coming to our
neighborhood soon. In fact, he may have already been here, disguised
as a rock-n-roll singer. His song was a call for us to get back to our
appropriate place, alongside of — NOT above — everyone else in
the human family.

Rock-n-rollers have taken up this prophetic role at several critical
moments in America's history: Bob Dylan in the 60s, Bruce Springsteen
in the 70s and 80s, Bono and U2 in the present day. Rock musicians
have exposed America's religious arrogance and self-serving theology time and time again, while so many in the Church have kept
silent. Take a look at the lyrics of Bob Dylan's "With God on Our
Side," Springsteen's "Born in the USA," or Pearl Jam's "Marker in the
Sand," and you'll see rock's prophets in action, doing the very work
that ministers, priests, imams, and rabbis should have been doing all
along. Dylan sang, "I's taught and brought up...that the land that I
live in has God on its side." He goes on to suggest sarcastically that
the Germans, who killed six million Jews, and even Judas Iscariot had
God on their side. (Bob Dylan, "With God on Our Side")

More than 40 years after Dylan's bitter ballad, Eddy Vedder and
Pearl Jam sang, "Now you got both sides claiming, killing in God's
name. But God is nowhere to be found..." Pearl Jam concludes their
prophetic call screaming, "What do you say? God, what do you say?"
It's as if this Seattle rock trio wants God to speak for Himself during
these tumultuous times, because so many of the religious folks, who
arrogantly assume God is on their side, are no longer to be trusted as
spokespersons for the Almighty.

Rock's prophets, throughout their five-decade history, have reminded
us again and again just how blind, nationalistic, and arrogant American
triumphant theology can be. Dylan's voice in "With God on Our Side" —
if we disregard its sarcastic tone — sounds frightfully similar to many
of today's religious fundamentalists, who operate completely out of
the unchallenged assumption that God *is* partial and that "we" *are* his

favorites. Yet Paul, in Acts 10:34, affirms that, "God does not show favoritism, but accepts people from every nation who revere Him and seek to do what is right."

It is time for everyone, regardless of religion, nationality, or political persuasion, to put away the "God is on our side" assumption once and for all. Jim Wallis's 2005 best seller, *God's Politics*, makes this point persuasively, but it should be noted prophetic rockers have been beating this same drum for a long, long time.

In Crosby, Stills, Nash, and Young's 1990s ironically titled, "American Dream," they sing of a nameless evangelist, a self-proclaimed model of American religious purity, who gets caught "with the girl next door and people's money piled on the floor." Crosby, Stills, Nash, and Young's story sounds eerily similar to Jesus' own teaching in Matthew 23:3-4, when he warns his true followers to beware of the Pharisees, "for they do not practice what they preach. They tie heavy loads and put them on men's shoulders, but they themselves are not willing to lift a finger to move them." Both Jesus and Crosby, Stills, Nash, and Young are lashing out at the same thing: those poor examples of faithful living who dare to point out the moral bankruptcy of others.

In Bruce Springsteen's bitterly sarcastic anthem, "Born in the U.S.A.," the Boss wonders how a country like ours can treat its own people — particularly its war veterans — the way the character in this song is treated. Can a country that leaves its own war veterans unemployed, unemployable, and on the streets, really claim to have God on its side? Neil Young blasts away at such American hypocrisy and callousness in "Keep on Rockin' in the Free World." He sings of a new mother who ends up "putting the kid away," in the trash dumpster, because of how hopeless her life has become here in the U.S. In a later verse, Young mocks a favorite expression of George H. Bush, singing "We got a thousand points of light for the homeless man," calling attention to the fact that America has turned its back on its poor, offering them nothing more than trite clichés and election-year sound bites. Young echoes the strains of the sixth century B.C.E. prophet, Amos, who castigated the Israelites for presuming to be God's chosen nation: "You who turn justice into bitterness and cast righteousness to the ground...You trample on the poor and force him to give you his grain...I know how many are your offenses and how great your sins." (Amos 5:6-12)

The late, great Johnny Cash spent his 50-year singing career dressed in black to call attention to the very injustices that so many of his fellow artists were clambering about: the poor, "the beaten down... and the ones who are held back." Cash closes his modern day prophetic text, better known as "The Man in Black," promising that "Til we start to make a move to make a few things right, you'll never see me wear a suit of white." Unfortunately, Cash died before he ever got to change the color of his clothing.

Rock songs like these and dozens of others have made me wonder if Jesus might have been speaking about the Rolling Stones when he said, in the Lukan account of the triumphal entry, "If they (his followers) keep quiet, the very *stones* will cry out!" (Luke 19:40)

In an attempt to combat the religious arrogance that lurks at the doorstep of my own church, I have come to refer, again and again, to Joshua chapter 5. At this critical crossroads in Israel's history, Joshua had just been handed the staff and mantle of leadership from Moses, just in time to lead the children of Israel across the Jordan River and into the Promised Land. Yet, a hornet's nest of political and religious battles awaited Joshua and the Jews there. In route to Jericho, Joshua sees an impressive man with his sword drawn, and soon discovers that it is none other than "the commander of the army of the Lord." Joshua can't resist the chance to get God on his side, as he and his troops head into battle. So Joshua asks, "Are you for us or for our enemies?" Then comes the reply that I wish would be painted on huge signs and waved in every packed football stadium, right alongside John 3:16: "Neither!" God's single-word answer to Joshua's small-minded, nationalistic question may be the most important and the most overlooked word in the entire canon... "Neither!" God's answer, when asked to pick sides, is always "Neither."

In their challenging and prophetic role, rock artists have consistently brought out the uncomfortable, yet undeniable, parallels between the Pharisees of the scriptures and we Americans — particularly American

Christians. It almost seems that our nation's rockers are more familiar with Joshua chapter 5 and God's resounding "Neither" than America's Christian leaders are! Thankfully, we find in the verses of Joshua 5 that follow the word "neither," that Joshua does eventually 'get it' and falls to his knees to ask the question he should have asked in the first place: "What message does my Lord have for his servant?" (Joshua 5:14) That's a long way from, 'Hey, God, are you on our side or theirs,' isn't it? Joshua eventually does what any and every person of faith should do when searching for the Holy One and a glimpse of His will. He dropped everything. He hit his knees and assumed the humble posture of a worshipful servant. Rather than continuing to jockey to get God on his side, Joshua simply asked, "What message does the Lord have for me today?"

Is Joshua's prayer — "What message do you have for me today, Lord?" — one that religious and spiritual people across this shrinking world, and particularly here in America, are saying? Or have most religious folks continued down the dangerous and blasphemous path of trying to get God on their side? I love the way that Bono put it when he addressed the National Prayer Breakfast back in February of '06.

> "For so much of my life, in countless ways, large and small, I was always seeking the Lord's blessing for what I was doing. I'd pray, 'God, I have this new song — look after it…I have a family, please look after them… I have this crazy idea…'But then I met a very wise man who said, 'Stop! Stop asking God to bless what *you're* doing! Get involved instead with what *God* is doing — because *that's already* blessed!'"
>
> – Bono
> (*www.data.org/archives/000774.php*)

Leave it to a rock-n-roller to bring us the Word of God with clarity, potency, and integrity.

Brothers and sisters, Muslims and Christians, Jews and Gentiles, Israelis and Palestinians, Shi'ites and Sunni's, while our religious and political leaders seem determined to divide us, rock-n-rollers are calling all of us to let go, once and for all, of the tempting, yet ultimately arrogant and heretical, assumption that God is, always has been, and always will be on our side. It is time that all of us, as Bono said, stop asking God to bless what we're doing, and instead throw 100-percent of our energy into finding out what God is already doing. If together we can find and ally ourselves with what God is up to, then perhaps God, through all of us, can save us from ourselves and further self-destruction.

Questioning God

"You're always letting us humans down, the
wars you wage, the babes you drown."
"Dear God" – XTC

If a European cartoon making light of Muhammad in 2006 can be grounds for Jihad, what might a song like XTC's "Dear God" incite? This 1986 release directly blames God for world hunger and injustice and goes on to call the Father, Son and Holy Ghost "just somebody's unholy hoax." Undoubtedly, there are those who would label such lyrics irreligious, sacrilegious, and even downright offensive. Call me a heretic (if you haven't already), but I see XTC's bitter prayer as inherently spiritual, giving voice to perfectly legitimate, authentic, and too often buried questions of faith. Their critique of an unseen and apparently inactive God dares to bring to the surface what most, if not all, believers can't help but wonder.

The singer refers to the Bible as written by "crazy humans," who are constantly "fighting in the street" because of their theological opinions. While such an attack on God, his word, and his people may seem blasphemous, it is actually a form of engagement with God that is included in the scriptures themselves. Read the Book of Job, over one-third of the Psalms, Ecclesiastes, and even the accounts of Jesus on the cross; people of faith have been questioning God and his goodness for at least 3,000 years.

Theologians call the kinds of questions XTC raises in their biting ballad "theodicy" questions. While many of us may not be familiar or comfortable with that heady term, we are all innately familiar with the questions of theodicy. They include: "How can a loving God cause or even allow his own creatures to suffer? Why do bad things happen to good people? How can entire populations and generations of innocent people be wiped off a planet that is supposedly in the hands of a loving God?"

The impulse to raise these kinds of questions is infinitely human, and thoughtful people of faith have wrestled with them since 1,000 B.C.E. and continue to do so today. I began struggling with theodicy as a child in the late 60s, watching the nightly news footage from Vietnam. I can still picture those endless, scrolling lists of dead soldiers — their names, ranks, and hometowns. From there, theodicy questions kept popping up for me whenever events like Jonestown, the Ethiopian famine, the genocide in Rwanda, 9/11, the Tsunami, and Katrina occurred. It was when I received a phone call on January 7, 2001 at 12:37 a.m., however, that this business of theodicy became personal for me. The caller informed me that my mother had been killed in a car crash, and that my father was in critical condition. The vehicle that struck my parents had been driven by a 16 year-old. He, too, was severely injured, while his 11-year old brother in the passenger seat was D.O.A.

The thing about theodicy questions, whether they're personal or global in nature, is that they don't come with answers, at least not satisfactory ones. That doesn't stop all kinds of well-intentioned believers from lining up to say things like, 'God has a reason for this,' and 'God never gives us more than we can handle.' For me, such bumper sticker theology and out-of-context, Hallmark Bible quoting always misses the mark. It missed the mark for Job as well, when his so-called "comforters" descended upon him in the wake of Job losing his wife, his children, his servants, his property, and all his livestock. Job's "comforters" said things to him like, "Is not your wickedness great? Are not your sins endless? You stripped men of their clothing, leaving them naked. You gave no water to the weary and you withheld food from the hungry…" (Job 22:5-7) Quite the bedside manner from Elihu here. Rarely does someone on the outside of a tragic situation have something biblically sound and emotionally sensitive to offer to one on the inside of suffering.

I have a real appreciation for what XTC does in "Dear God." Their song seems to come from inside the reality of suffering. The singer has seen, heard, and had enough of starvation, shipwrecks, drownings, diseases, and religious fighting. XTC's existential anger is not only brutally honest, but markedly similar to Job's. Remember when the biblical sufferer cried,

> "How I long for the months gone by, for the days when God watched over me…when the Almighty was still with me… For now men mock me in song; I have become a byword among them. They detest me and keep their distance; they do not hesitate to spit in my face. Now that God has unstrung my bow and afflicted me, they throw off restraint in my presence."
>
> (Job 29:1-5, 30:9-11)

If Job had been familiar with the 1980s hair band, Twisted Sister, he might have used their immortal words: "We're not gonna take it!" XTC is saying the same thing, and they're saying it directly to God. Many of us aren't used to that kind of candor in front of the Almighty, despite Job's example.

Christians in particular are not well schooled in the Hebrew practice of lamentation, and so when we encounter it, be it in the Book of Job or in an XTC song, it feels inappropriate and disrespectful. Yet XTC feels no such discomfort and wastes no time taking off the gloves to climb into the ring with God. The British rockers use the second person "you" throughout the song, so there is no mistaking whom they are attacking: "It's you, dear god!"

The parallels between "Dear God" and the Judeo-Christian scriptures don't end with Job. There's a cynicism in XTC that is reminiscent of Qoheleth, the author of Ecclesiastes, whose letter begins, "Meaningless! Meaningless!" says the Teacher. "Utterly meaningless! Everything is meaningless. What does a man gain from all his labor at which he toils under the sun?" (Eccles. 1:1-3) In chapter six, Qoheleth goes on to say, "God gives a man wealth and possessions and honor, so that he lacks nothing his heart desires, but God does not enable him to enjoy them...This is meaningless, a grievous evil." The ancient preacher paints God as cruel here, as one who taunts us with a taste of contentment, only to rip it right out of our mouths. (Eccles 6:2) And, to further question God's ways, Qoheleth adds, "In this meaningless life of mine, I have seen both of these: a righteous man perishing in his righteousness, and a wicked man living long in his wickedness." Here, within the very canon of scripture, Qoheleth calls God unfair. He concludes that in a God-run universe, righteousness is not rewarded and wickedness is not punished. Job raised the same questions and received no satisfactory answers. Ecclesiastes offers us no resolution either.

Given what biblical scholars tell us about the canonical process, we might ask why books like Job and Ecclesiastes were not kept out of the canon. The early Church must have felt that they offered something of spiritual value. For me, Job and Ecclesiastes are two of the most honest, human books in the testaments, giving voice to universal and inexplicable human experiences. We learn from all these scriptural voices that our faith in God does not shield us from suffering, from loss, nor from any of the other things Job, himself, experienced. XTC's "Dear God," therefore, has a place in a collection of spiritual songs, because it reminds all spiritual seekers of the important truth that faith in God does not answer all questions, explain away every unspeakable evil, nor put an end to theodicy — theology's stickiest wicket.

XTC is not alone in using the platform of rock stardom to join in the theodicy chorus. Long time rock legend, Neil Young, engages in theodicy in one of his most recent records, *Prairie Wind*. On a track called "When God Made Me," Neil raises a plethora of questions that might seem inappropriate or disrespectful to some religious devotees. He wonders if God envisioned "all the wars…fought in his name" and whether there is "only one way to be close to" God. Toward the song's end, Neil even goes after the tricky, somewhat contradictory notion of free will, asking, "Did He give me the gift of vision not knowing what I might see?"

Randy Newman turned up the heat on theodicy by writing a song from God's perspective, depicting the Lord as critical of the simple-minded folk who believe in Him. "Blind" and "crazy to put your faith in me," are just a few of the jabs Newman takes at believers, as he paints God as both callous and condescending. Newman's final request to this somewhat evil God is "if you won't take care of us, won't you please just let us be?" (Randy Newman, "God's Song")

No group in human history has had more cause to wonder why God "won't take care" of them than the Jews. When holocaust survivor Elie Wiesel wrote *Night,* he chronicled his own struggle with theodicy, initially in the form of a lament, but eventually in an even more hostile, accusatory way than any of the aforementioned rockers did. Young Elie was an eyewitness to the Nazi atrocities, as they played out perilously close to him. After witnessing one particularly brutal hanging — of a young child — Wiesel says of God,

> "Why should I bless Him?… Because He had had thousands of children burned in His pits? Because He kept six crematories working night and day, on Sundays and feast days? Because in His great might He had created Aushwitz, Birkenau, Buna, and so many factories of death? How could I say to Him: 'Blessed art Thou, Eternal, Master of the Universe, Who chose us from among the races to be tortured day and night, to see our fathers, our mothers, our brothers, end in the crematory?" Wiesel concludes, "On this day I had ceased to plead. I was no longer capable of lamentation. On the contrary, I felt very strong. I was the accuser, God the accused. My eyes were open and I was alone — terribly alone in a world without God and without man. Without love or mercy.

I had ceased to be anything but ashes, yet I felt myself
to be stronger than the Almighty, to whom my life had
been tied for so long."
(Elie Wiesel, *Night*, Bantam Books, 1960, pgs. 64–5)

Was Wiesel leaving Judaism and abandoning his faith as he endured
the holocaust and then wrote about it so frankly? No! No more than
Jesus was abandoning his faith in his Father when he uttered his own
cry of dereliction from the cross, saying, "My God, my God, why have
You forsaken me?" (Mark 15:34) Jesus was dealing honestly and passionately with the brutal truth that he was experiencing, just as Wiesel
dealt honestly and passionately with the horrors that came his way in
a Nazi concentration camp.

Authentic people of faith, including the Son of Man, himself, are
not immune from experiencing the horrors of humanity. Why should
the God we worship be immune to or protected from our anger, our
confusion, or our righteous indignation in the face of cruel, unjust,
and inexplicable suffering? It's a shame that in an era like ours, so full
of injustice and unthinkable suffering, people of faith have lost touch
with the one biblical form we were given to express our struggles with
theodicy: the lament. Despite Job's example, the witness of Qoheleth in
Ecclesiastes, and the words of Jesus himself on the cross, it may take an
irreverent rock-n-roll band like XTC, Randy Newman, or Neil Young
to reconnect us with one of our own forgotten biblical practices.

These honest, courageous rockers, who called God's justice into
question, were speaking for many of us who live on this side of the
great divide that separates man from God. In raising such questions,
rockers were not terminating their relationship with God; for they
were still communicating with Him, still struggling with Him, still
expressing themselves to Him. Despite the seemingly disrespectful
and attacking tone rockers have taken in their musical expressions
of theodicy, these prophetic bards show that they still believe in God
enough to yell at Him and to question his ways. May the conversation continue…

Brotherly Love

"*No burden is he...He ain't heavy; he's my brother.*"
"He Ain't Heavy, He's My Brother" – The Hollies

In one of my favorite novels of all time, *A River Runs Through It*, Norman MacLean shows us just how complicated and gut-wrenching our family ties can be. Paul, the younger and wayward brother in MacLean's fictional family, becomes the heaviest burden his parents and older brother have ever borne. Paul MacLean bears a striking similarity to the prodigal son Jesus spoke of in his famous parable. (Luke 15:11-32) The younger brother in Jesus' story demands his share of his inheritance while his father is still alive. Taking the money, the prodigal leaves his older brother alone in his father's field with twice as much work to do, while the younger goes off on a hedonistic bender that lands him broke, starving, and living in a pig's sty. When this wayward son "comes to his senses" and realizes that, "many of my father's servants have bread enough and to spare," he heads for home with a well-rehearsed 'forgive me' speech in his

43

pocket. With a merciful father and an embittered brother awaiting him, the stage is set for a family feud of Biblical proportions.

Bruce Springsteen, one of rock's premier spiritual voices of the last 50 years, brings this same theme of familial tension to life in his haunting ballad, "Highway Patrolman." Frank and Joe Roberts play out for us the messiness of brotherly love and test the murky limits of human forgiveness. These "blood on blood" brothers had some great times together, "laughing and drinking," and "dancing with Maria." But when Franky started "strayin'" and turning "his back on his family," the weight of brotherly love begins to sink in.

It's an old, old story, told and retold in the canon of literature, film, and Holy Scripture. Cain and Abel, Jacob and Esau, Joseph and his 11 brothers, Norman MacLean, Springsteen, and Jesus all wrestle with the same essential story, a story of betrayal and pain, all in the fragile context of what we've come to call family.

How tough it is to live together in some semblance of harmony, even with those we love most. Whenever I work with families in conflict, I tell them that Don Henley is closer to the truth about what makes relationships work than The Beatles were. Lennon and McCartney claimed that, "all you need is love." Henley, on the other hand, said that forgiveness was at "the heart of the matter." Given our human frailties, imperfections, and tendency toward sin, I've come to believe that forgiveness really is the single most important ingredient in any relationship. "We all need a little tenderness...in such a graceless age...I think it's about forgiveness, forgiveness." (Don Henley, "The Heart of the Matter")

Peter once asked Jesus, "Lord, how many times must I forgive my brother when he sins against me — as many as seven times?" Jesus replied, "I tell you, not seven but seventy seven times." (Matthew 18:21-22) But Jesus' mathematical words here are much easier said than done, particularly when it comes to those with whom we live day in and day out. With my own family, I am much more like the embittered older brother in the prodigal son parable than I am the grace-filled, forgiving father. It has always bothered me that I can be so quick to extend grace and Christ-like forgiveness to strangers and so slow to offer it to my own blood relatives. The Seattle-based rock trio, Pearl Jam, is on target in their latest release, "Marker in the Sand," when they describe humans as "so unforgiving, yet needing forgiveness first."

Springsteen's "Highway Patrolman," Joe Roberts, has had to forgive his brother Frank repeatedly, bailing him out of situation after situation. Frank's constant straying puts an unbearable strain on their relationship. When Frank finally kills a man and Joe gets the call on the shortwave to chase the fleeing Frank, we are all left wondering, right along with Joe, whether there's a limit to brotherly love. Is there a line a brother can cross that justifies the rest of his family turning their backs on him? "How many times must I forgive my brother when he sins against me?"

A friend of mine has a son who has flunked out and been kicked out of a half-dozen schools — public and private. His son has been caught with drugs, stolen property, and has even ripped off his own father to the tune of thousands of dollars. My friend has agonized over what to do with his prodigal son. His second marriage was being dragged down the tubes by the weight of his son's behavior. His second wife and many wise friends counseled him to cut his boy loose and kick him out of the house. Like Joe Roberts in the Springsteen song, my friend just couldn't pull that trigger. He'd stood by his son in all circumstances, as any good father would try to do. No matter what legal or moral lines his boy crossed, he has never been able to get himself to that point of concluding resolutely what Springsteen's Joe Roberts tries to: that his own boy, his own flesh and blood, "ain't no damn good." (Bruce Springsteen, "Highway Patrolman")

Certainly, seeing his own child make one self-destructive decision after another made my friend want to give up at times, particularly as his prodigal got older and the cost of his mistakes increased exponentially. Yet, this is a father who takes his cues from Jesus, and followers of the Nazarene have an added pressure to welcome home their prodigal sons and daughters again and again, no matter how often or how badly their children stray. The list of scoundrels to whom Jesus gave chance after chance is long and well documented. Look at Peter; he is the "rock" on whom Jesus would eventually build His church.

In the end, there are no clear limits or boundaries when it comes to loving and forgiving our brothers and sisters. In the final pages of *A River Runs Through It,* the father speaks to his older son about the younger, prodigal son, Paul, who had just been killed in a bar fight. The bar fight was only the latest in a life filled with dangerous and self-destructive choices Paul had made. The father asks, "Do you think I could have helped him?" The older brother thinks to himself and confesses to the reader that, "Even if I might have thought longer, I would have made the same answer." Then he returns the same question to his dad, "Do you think I could have helped him?" "…We stood waiting in deference to each other. How can a question be answered that asks a lifetime of questions?" The father eventually concludes that, "It is those we live with and love and should know who elude us." (MacLean, *A River Runs Through It,* University of Chicago Press, 1976, pgs. 103–4)

As Springsteen's "Highway Patrolman" draws to a close, Frankie eludes his brother Joe, the one who had loved and known him best. As to whether that patrolman brother "pulled over to the side of the highway and watched his (Frank's) taillights disappear" because he wasn't able to catch up, or because Joe had simply chosen, once again, to let Frank off the hook, Springsteen isn't clear. And that is as it should be; for when it comes to loving and forgiving our brothers, nothing ever is.

Caring for the Environment

"We are stardust, we are golden. . .and we've got to get ourselves back to the garden."
"Woodstock" – Joni Mitchell

I remember being in my friend's tree fort when I was 11, listening to AM radio, when Cat Stevens' "Where Do the Children Play" came on. While I didn't grasp all of the song's richness back then, I do remember being saddened by his depiction of a future where all the open, green, play space had been turned into concrete. Stevens envisioned a world with no place left to build but up, "higher and higher," until "there's no more room up there." Thirty-five years later, I live in the world Stevens foresaw, the cluttered, concrete world, where my own children have no place left to play.

At the 2007 Grammy awards, Vice President Al Gore was a presenter, and he began by thanking the rock music community for always being at the forefront of the environmental movement. That truly is where rock artists have been throughout my entire life, for I've heard and learned more about the environment from rock-n-roll musicians than

I ever have from pastors and church leaders. In most local churches, we're lucky to get the obligatory Earth Day sermon in mid-April. Other than that, the only trace of environmentalism we might find in a church is some hippie in Birkenstocks urging the ladies in the fellowship hall to use real cups instead of Styrofoam at the coffee hour. By and large, the Christian church has been conspicuously silent when it comes to taking care of the earth, the planet they insist that God created.

From very early in rock's history, its artists have recognized the power and beauty of the earth and have sung its praises. Cat Stevens took a religious hymn, "Morning has Broken," with lyrics like "God's recreation of the new day" and turned it into a top 40 hit. The Woodstock Festival was a massive celebration not only of rock music, but of land, sky, water, and air. Joni Mitchell's ode to that gathering spoke of coming "upon a child of God" and "going down to Yasgur's farm," where one could "get back to the land and set" her "soul free." The hundreds of thousands in that rock congregation were outdoors, intentionally unprotected from the elements, both the hot sun and the drenching downpours. Even the mud at Woodstock was received as a gift, a slippery playground, a glimpse of "the garden" Mitchell called us back to, a clear and direct reference to the Garden of Eden in Genesis 1 and 2.

Activist Bruce Cockburn is another rocker who has offered praise to creation in his upbeat "Goin' to the Country." The song's opening "da-da-da-da-da's" hint at a beauty and a joy beyond words, and from there, Cockburn needs only to look out his window to notice cows, trees, birds, and the sunshine that "smiles on me." All that Cockburn sees prompts him to move closer, to get out into the midst of all this beauty, to go into "the country," where he can smell the grass and be "happy as can be."

One can almost hear traces of Psalm 8 in "Morning has Broken," "Woodstock," and "Goin' to the Country." In that famous creation hymn, the Psalmist "considers the works" of the Creator's hands, "the moon and the stars," "the flocks and herds," "the birds of the air and the fish of the sea," and concludes, "O Lord, our Lord, how majestic is your name in all the earth." (Psalm 8:3-9)

Not only have Rock musicians praised creation, but they have been equally biblical in the attention they've paid to fallen creation, to man's chronic mistreatment of the planet, and to the need for us to restore our proper relationship to it. Al Gore may have brought Global Warming back into the public debate with his 2006 release, "An Inconvenient Truth," but bands like Midnight Oil have been singing about climate change for decades. Back then, however, few, if any, of us were listening. In "Beds are Burning," the angry boys from Down Under screamed for us to face the "facts," and to give the earth back to whom it belongs. "How do we sleep when our beds are burning?" Stephen Stills' 1991 solo release, *Stills Alone,* contains a powerful indictment of man's abuse of the Amazon rain forest. "In the time it takes to sing this song," notes Stills, "another acre gone, Amazonia." He goes on to say that we've got to "save the rain forest from ourselves." (Stephen Stills, "Amazonia")

As far back as Genesis chapter three, humans are confronted with the enmity we've created between ourselves and the earth. "Cursed is the ground because of you," and "the Lord God banished Adam from the Garden of Eden to work the ground."(Gen. 3:17, 23) In the Torah, God's people are reminded of God's desire to protect the earth when He commands, "Do not pollute the land where you are." (Numbers 35:33) As Biblical history unfolds, we humans consistently disregard God's will for peace and harmony in our relationship with the earth, leading God to send Isaiah with the prophesy, "My righteousness draws near speedily...and my arm will bring justice to the nations...the heavens will vanish like smoke, the earth will wear out like a garment and its inhabitants die like flies." (Isaiah 51:6) Jesus, himself, foretold of similar environmental crises in Luke 21. "There will be great earthquakes, famines, and pestilences in various places, and fearful events and great signs from heaven...There will be signs in the sun, moon, and stars...the roaring and tossing of the sea." (Luke 21:11, 25) In 2007, these words of the Nazarene ring truer than ever. The earth has, indeed, become like an old, worn out garment, with holes in its neck and tears in its sleeves. We humans are only beginning to understand that we can't simply buy a new environment; there is no replacing this earth with another one.

Thankfully, rockers have done much more than simply condemn our mistreatment of the earth. They have called us to a more responsible stewardship of the planet and to an awareness of the effects our polluting behavior will have on future generations. Kenny Loggins, in "Conviction of the Heart," calls us to change our ways. He notes that we've already created air "too angry to breath" and water "our children can't drink." Loggins' conviction is that we are all one "with the earth, with the sky, with everything in life," and he calls us to act with conviction, so that we might leave our children a safe, clean, and sustainable world. Graham Nash's "Clear Blue Skies" begins asking a question about the skies and their current condition. He then moves to water, posing the question of whether it's too much to ask of us that we leave our children and grandchildren clean water. He closes the tune wondering whether any of the vital sources that were here when we came "will be here when we're gone?"

Perhaps nowhere is rock's environmental call so clear, so profound, and so blatantly biblical as in the aforementioned "Woodstock" by Joni Mitchell. "We are stardust, we are golden… and we've got to get ourselves back to the garden." Mitchell's allusion to Eden is both obvious and indisputable. She understands the created order all too well, from God's gracious plan and provisions, to the human abandonment of God's intended harmony between man and nature. Mitchell calls us back to garden living, to harmony with one another and with nature, and an entire generation resonated with her call. The Apostle Paul put it this way: "For the whole creation waits in eager expectation…the whole creation has been groaning as in the pains of childbirth right up to the present time." (Romans 5:19, 22) Paul's double emphasis on "the whole creation" is targeted to all those who assume that Christ came only to redeem and save people. Biblical salvation is about much more than mere personal, human salvation; it is a salvation for the very earth itself and for all that God created, because it all needs saving.

Why have so many proponents of Christianity been so uninterested and under involved in the environmental movement? A subtle but significant error in biblical interpretation is, at least in part, to blame. I call it 'the heresy of heaven,' that long-standing notion that God's people are only temporarily visiting this planet, that their true home and eventual place of residence is elsewhere — out there, up there, far away from here. The Apostle Paul may have helped sow the seeds of this heresy when he called Christians "aliens and strangers on earth," who have their citizenship "in heaven." (Philippians 3:20, Hebrews 11:13-14) But one of the most basic principles of New Testament hermeneutics is never to give undue emphasis to an individual, isolated verse, particularly when it is taken out of context. A second crucial interpretive principle for Christians is that the life and teaching of Jesus should always supersede other voices. When it comes to Jesus' teachings about "the Kingdom of God," there is a preponderance of evidence that Jesus was far more interested in this world than in the next.

Rob Bell, founding pastor of the amazing Mars Hill Community in Grandville, Michigan, argues that the original Greek text proves that Jesus rarely if ever even used the word "heaven." Instead, says Bell, Jesus consistently spoke of "the age to come," a time — not a place — when his kingdom principles would be lived out. (Rob Bell, from the "Isn't She Beautiful" conference for pastors, at Mars Hill Bible Church, 1/22/07) To bolster Bell's argument, we should remember that Jesus taught us to pray, "Thy kingdom come, Thy will be done on earth…" (Matthew 6:10) On the day Jesus called Zacchaeus out of the Sycamore tree and went to his home, Jesus said, "Today salvation has come to your house." Zacchaeus' response to Jesus' presence was a pledge to give half his wealth to the poor and to repay, four-fold, all those he had defrauded in his tax collecting business. Zacchaeus's pledge was for this life, not the next. The proof of Zacchaeus' salvation, therefore, is found in the changes he makes in his life here and now.

Yet, so many Bible-banging followers of Christ continue to insist that the essence of Christianity lies in getting souls to heaven. Those who have seen the documentary *Jesus Camp* or have taken evangelism training courses from any number of para-church and mega-church organizations know that the heresy of heaven is alive and well. Well-intentioned evangelicals ask total strangers on the street, their own relatives, and even elementary school children the same initial question: "If you were to die tonight, would you be certain that you'd be admitted to heaven?" This approach to 'sharing the faith' is based on a false and highly individualistic understanding of salvation, one that has reduced Jesus to a ticket-master outlet, whose sole purpose is to provide backstage passes to heaven. Only those carrying the right spiritual currency will be allowed into the kingdom. Once salvation and Jesus' purpose get reduced to transporting souls to the after life, it's only a matter of time until life here and now — and the environment that sustains it — becomes utterly unimportant.

The implications of this heretical reductionism are far-reaching and horrifying, and we're feeling their effects every day. The Edge, guitarist for U2, put it this way: "The reliance on the fairy tale pie in the sky when you die aspect of religion is dangerous, because it excuses so much... Our stance as a band is that we believe in heaven, but we live as if we didn't." (*U2 by U2*, Harper Collins, 2006, p. 299)

If one takes the time to look at how the Bible both begins and ends, he will see quite quickly that the unfolding story of salvation history takes place here on earth. It begins with a garden in Genesis 1, and it ends, in Revelation 21 and 22, NOT with the good guys being beamed up to some heavenly realm, but, instead, with the Son of God coming down to earth, bringing with him the "New Jerusalem." The end of the biblical story tells of the restoration of *all* creation here on earth. The planet is renewed and reconstituted in accordance with God's kingdom principles. The voice from God's descending throne says, "Now the dwelling of God is with men, and He will live with them." (Rev 21:3) This is hardly the picture painted by Hal Lindsay and the *Left Behind films*.

Salvation, as Jesus understood it, was the process through which one begins living according to kingdom or "age to come" principles here on the earth, here and now, even before the age to come actually arrives. I believe it was German philosopher and theologian Simone Weil who called the Christian life 'living as if.' To Weil, a Christian or a 'saved' person was one who went ahead and lived — here and now — according to the kingdom of God principles that Jesus laid out in his three-year ministry.

When it comes to the environment and the biblical concept of salvation, once again we find that secular rock singers have been closer to the truth of Jesus than many of those who call themselves Christians. In praising creation, railing against the human mistreatment of the earth, and calling us to work toward its restoration, rockers have been right in line with the biblical paradigm.

Toward the end of his profound and prolific musical career, John Lennon wrote a song called "Imagine," in which he asked us to "imagine there's no heaven." As has so often been the case with prophetic rock artists, Lennon was practically crucified by the religious establishment for his 'atheistic,' 'anti-religious' beliefs. Yet, if we really listen to the lyrics of "Imagine," we can't help but see that what Lennon was truly after was the entire creation living in harmony, "as one." Far from lambasting or belittling Christian beliefs in "Imagine," Lennon was looking for a way to deepen and enhance people's commitment to this life, to this world, and to the earth. He saw no benefit in people writing off this planet, as if it were nothing more than a temporary stop en route to some other worldly destination.

In Genesis 1:26, the biblical writers depict God as giving humans "dominion" over the earth and the command to "fill the earth" and "subdue it." While so many religious humans have taken this verse as license to do with the earth whatever they want, those of us who have studied biblical Hebrew know better. The Hebrew word "radah," which is often translated as "have dominion over," would be better translated "be a responsible steward with." The Hebrew, in other words, conveys an understanding that the earth does not belong to us, the same insight that Midnight Oil tried to convey in "Beds are Burning:" "it belongs to them, we've got to give it back."

Jesus' parable of the tenants in Matthew 21:33-40 is a helpful passage to consider at this point. The owner of the vineyard entrusts his property to the care of stewards while he must be away. The longer the owner is away, the more the stewards lose sight of the intended arrangement and begin to use the vineyard to their own ends rather than the master's. They abuse it, claim its fruits and profits for themselves, and ultimately kill the master's son. As with so many of Jesus' parables, this one is as shockingly true today as it was 2000 years ago in terms of how we have corrupted our relationship with God's earth.

I am grateful to the many rockers who have, intentionally or unintentionally, steered me toward a more biblical and godly approach to my relationship with the earth and with the rest of God's creation. In my forty-five years in the church, I've learned next to nothing about environmental stewardship. Were it not for rock's positive and spiritual influence, I'd still be sipping coffee out of a Styrofoam cup in my church's fellowship hall.

Growing Old

"So scared of getting older, I'm only good at being young."'
"Stop This Train" – John Mayer

Rock music has long been associated with youth. While each generation since Elvis's has had its own version of rock-n-roll, all of rock's generations have been united in defining themselves in opposition to parents and the establishment. In The Who's classic, "My Generation," Roger Daltry summarized what many believe to be rock's entire take on aging: "I hope I die before I get old." Another anti-aging lyric that many rock stars seem to have taken literally is Neil Young's "it's better to burn out than it is to rust." (Neil Young, "Hey, Hey, My, My") Given rock's tendency to be the mouthpiece of the young, it would be easy to assume rock has nothing valuable to say about growing old (beyond simply protesting it). The fact is, however, many rock lyrics have been both profound and surprisingly insightful in their reflection upon the aging process.

In many of rock's reflections on aging, artists have dealt head on with the fact that our days are numbered and that life is finite. On their hugely successful 80s effort, *Daylight Again*, Crosby, Stills and

Nash included a tune entitled "Might as Well Have a Good Time." Its refrain says, "It ain't long before it's gone. Might as well have a good time." In Warren Zevon's *The Wind*, the record he made while dying of lung cancer, he sings a raucous tune called "The Rest of the Night," in which he asks, "Why stop now?" and then yells, "We may never get this chance again, let's party for the rest of the night!" It's the cry of a man who knows how precious time is, how fleeting his days and nights have become.

While it's understandable that some would interpret such songs as hedonistic and short-sighted, advocating a 'live for the moment' ethic, it is equally possible that these tunes are modern versions of what Qoheleth, the Old Testament author of Ecclesiastes, wrote thousands of years ago. "A man can do nothing better than to eat and drink and find satisfaction in his work…I know that there is nothing better for men than to be happy and do good while they live." (Ecclesiastes 2:25, 3:12-13) The Psalmist adds to this same theme, saying, "The length of our days is seventy years — or eighty if we have the strength…they quickly pass and we fly away." (Psalm 90:10) Even Jesus himself once said, "Do not worry about tomorrow, for tomorrow will worry about itself." (Matthew 6:34) Such a preponderance of biblical material calling us to be fully engaged in the present moment could be misconstrued as some sort of divine sanctioning of hedonism. In truth, the biblical writers and Jesus are far more likely to be reminding us of the deep, godly truth that our days are limited and that we ought to treasure each and every moment. Many rock lyricists have sung of the very same thing.

While some rockers seem hell-bent on fighting off the aging process, slowing it down, or even denying it altogether, other more mature voices have looked squarely at the inevitability of growing up, growing old, and even growing sentimental about the days gone by. "Yesterday all my troubles seem so far away, now it looks as though they're here to stay," said Paul McCartney at age 19. At an even earlier age, the great Neil Young understood that "you can't be twenty on Sugar Mountain," his metaphor for childhood. Neil knew that growing up, growing old, and growing into new responsibilities happens whether one is ready or not. Barenaked Ladies made this same point, albeit less poetically, in their 1990s hit "Baby Seat," singing, "You can't live your life in the baby seat. You've got to stand on your own." The rest of the song chides those who shirk responsibility and are not "grown up enough." Crash Test Dummies offered a more light-hearted look at the less-than-thrilling prospects that lay before them in their golden years. In their 90s hit, "Afternoons and Coffee Spoons," these offbeat Canadian rockers acknowledged that, "Someday I'll have a disappearing hairline," and "wear pajamas in the day time." They sang of doctors, prescriptions, and a desire to "change the test results" future physical exams might bring.

As recently as 2007, John Mayer struck Grammy gold with his *Continuum* CD. That profound record contains a soon-to-be hit single entitled "Stop This Train," which compares time to a speeding train, catapulting Mayer (and all of us) into a future for which he is not ready. "So scared of getting older, I'm only good at being young." Eventually, in the song's final verse, Mayer's dad tries to help young John come to terms with the fact that there is no stopping the train of aging, that, literally as well as metaphorically, there is no going back.

Again, the preacher Qoheleth tried to bring people of faith to this same acceptance and understanding in the wisdom-packed book of Ecclesiastes. In the book's most famous chapter, he penned what many still think came from Roger McGwinn and The Byrds:

> There is a time for everything
>   and a season for every matter under heaven:
> a time to be born and a time to die,
> a time to plant and a time to pluck up what is planted,
> a time to kill and a time to heal,
> a time to tear down and a time to build,
> a time to weep and a time to laugh,
> a time to mourn and a time to dance,
> a time to scatter stones and a time to gather stones together,
> a time to embrace and a time to refrain from embracing,
> a time to search and a time to give up searching,
> a time to keep and a time to give away,
> a time to tear and a time to mend,

a time to be silent and a time to speak,
a time to love and a time to hate,
a time for war and a time for peace.
— Ecclesiastes 3:1-8

Rock's surprisingly sensitive and spiritual treatment of aging also includes songs that reveal our society's tendency to discard those who have lost their youth. The Beatles asked the painful question, "Will you still need me, will you still feed me when I'm 64?" To have these mop-topped kids, so representative of all that is young, contemplating a time when they would have thinning hair and potentially be cast out by the women in their lives shows not only a real maturity on their part, but also gives us a clear indication that not all rock singers would rather die than get old.

Bruce Springsteen also reflected on how his life down aging's road might look in "Glory Days." The Boss had been around too many people who lived in the past to ever want to become one of them. "Hope when I get older I don't sit around trying to recapture…the glory, 'cause time passes by and leaves you with nothing…but boring stories…" Springsteen is one of many rockers who realized that one who lives his later years constantly looking back is wasting the particular gifts that longevity offers.

Rock's most poignant treatment of the aging process comes from Ben Folds. His ballad "Fred Jones, Part II" is a stunning look at a man, who is let go by the newspaper he had served so loyally for 25 years. It seems that before Mr. Jones is escorted out of his office by someone who doesn't even know his first name, Jones has already been replaced, quickly and heartlessly, by the machinery of the corporate world. As Folds puts it, "he's forgotten but not yet gone." Folds' brutal look at what has become all-too-common in today's downsizing world would have provided the perfect soundtrack for the film *About Schmidt*, another stunningly sensitive secular portrayal of aging in America, starring Jack Nicholson.

Many of the great biblical characters struggled with growing old in the same ways that these rock characters have. Abraham and Sarah longed for a child their entire lives. When Abraham was 75,

God came to him promising not only a son, but an entire nation of offspring (Gen.12:2). This promise, however, was only the beginning of a long and perilous journey Abraham and Sarah would so faithfully take. Despite them leaving their home and country, facing risks to their lives, and challenges to their old bodies, God's promise went unfulfilled for more than 20 years. Abraham then cried out to God, "You have given me no children!" (Gen. 15:3) Finally, at 99 years of age, Abraham receives word from God that he and Sarah will have their long-awaited child. All Abraham could do at this point was laugh at this preposterous notion. "Abraham fell face down; he laughed, saying to himself, 'Will a son be born to a man a hundred years old? Will Sarah bear a child at the age of 90?'" (Genesis 17:17) The promised son does come, but only after Abraham and Sarah have endured some of old age's harshest realities.

When we think of Moses, we tend to focus first on his heroic leadership guiding the Israelites out of Egypt and out of their enslavement to Pharoah. We often forget that Moses, himself, never got to enter the Promised Land. The very man God used to lead this land-less nation through 40 years of desert wandering was forbidden to cross the Jordan and to enter the land that flowed with milk and honey. Deuteronomy 34 reports that,

> "Then Moses climbed Mount Nebo...and there the Lord showed him the whole land...Then the Lord said to him: 'This is the land I promised on oath to Abraham, Isaac, and Jacob...I have let you see it with your eyes, but you will not cross over into it.' And then Moses, the servant of the Lord, died right there in Moab."
>
> (Deut. 34:1-5)

How unfair! Of all the Israelites who most deserved to enter this long-awaited land, Moses was at the top of the list. Yet, like Fred Jones, Moses finds himself replaced by a much younger man and laid to rest rather unceremoniously.

We can't leave out Job when considering the Bible's treatment of the aging process. Job was a highly successful farmer, with enormous acreage, a large family, and more livestock than most other characters in the scriptures. Yet, later in Job's life, tragedies were heaped upon him, everything from natural disasters to murderous raids upon his family and animals. He sees God as having "stripped (him) of (his) honor." Job feels "alienated" and "estranged" from both family and friends. Physically, he is described as "nothing but skin and bones." All that Job worked for in his youth was taken from him later in life, and though he cried out to God about it, he tells his comforters that, "I get no response." (Job 19:7-22)

So, in Abraham, Moses, and Job, we see the Bible's willingness to look unflinchingly at the ravages that await us as we age, just as rockers from Ben Folds to the Beatles have. The canons of both Christianity and rock-n-roll have helped me confront and deal with my own march through the aging process. I was barely thirty when my hairline retreated, as if being pursued by an advancing army. Not long after baldness set in, I began to experience the joys of hemorrhoids and suppositories. (Did they really have to make them look like silver bullets?) At age 40, the unthinkable happened; my lithe 170-pound frame began to yield to my inner balloon. By 45 I had shattered the 200-pound barrier, despite all kinds of dieting and exercise. In the next couple years, I will have both hips replaced, and if the bags under my eyes get any bigger, they may find themselves sponsored by Samsonite. On a more serious note, in my middle age years, I've lost friends to cancer, to AIDS, and to the war on terror. I have also been diagnosed with depression, an extremely tough pill for me to swallow. Somehow, both my Christian faith and my constant immersion in rock-n-roll music have helped me age with a sense of humor, a balanced perspective, and a measure of grace.

Thankfully, both rock and the Bible do more than simply chronicle the perils of aging; they help us come to terms with it and keep it in perspective. Paul Simon's "Still Crazy After All These Years" is a wonderful and balanced look at how we can embrace our own aging. Simon's narrator in "Still Crazy" runs into an old lover and the two "talked about some old times" and "drank (themselves) some beers." He "never worries," recognizing that "it's all going to fade." The refrain, "Still crazy after all these years," is Simon's wistful, reflective, and humorous look at himself. In him, we see the possibility of adopting such a perspective for ourselves as well.

Similarly, the Grateful Dead's highest chart climber, "Touch of Gray," is an attempt to make peace with the inevitable aging process. Jerry Garcia makes fun of himself and the state of his life, his relationships, and even his house, as he grows old. The rent hasn't been paid, the dog hasn't been fed, his 17 year-old kid can't read, "but it's alright." As the final chorus comes around, Garcia notes that, "a touch of gray kind of suits you anyway." Despite all the challenges and hardships of aging, Garcia knows that he'll survive it, and if he can, so can we.

James Taylor adds his voice to rock's collective wisdom on aging in "The Secret o' Life." For JT, aging is just a part of the process of life, a part of the journey. Taylor is neither fighting off the onset of aging, nor railing against time's passage. He accepts it as a part of the natural course of things. His advice is that we "enjoy the ride," "open our hearts," and recognize that "we're only here for a while." Life, at its core, says Taylor, is "a lovely ride," a mystery that even Einstein never fully understood.

Warren Zevon, who is most famous for his youthful sarcasm and dark humor in "Werewolves of London," "Excitable Boy," and "Lawyers, Guns, and Money," came to a point where he faced not only the onset of aging, but his own impending death as well. Diagnosed with lung cancer in its final stages, Zevon refused treatment and went into the studio, in the six months doctors speculated that he had left, to write and record one last record with his closest musical friends. His final album, fittingly entitled *The Wind*, used his last breaths to sing about what mattered to him most. One of the tracks focuses on the universal desire to be remembered after we die. He sings of "running out of breath," and asks repeatedly that we "keep (him) in our heart for awhile." Zevon believed that once he passed, we would still be able to think of him while "doing simple things around the house." While "Keep Me in Your Heart" is a tremendously sad song, Zevon takes consolation in the fact that his loved ones will keep him alive in their hearts, their thoughts, and their dreams.

The very first Sunday after hearing Zevon's "Keep Me in Your Heart," I played his song during my congregation's celebration of communion. Many in the congregation were moved to tears, as they came forward for the body and blood of Christ, with Zevon singing "Keep me in your heart for a while." The parallels between his emotions at life's end and Christ's were unmistakable. As a pastor who has conducted dozens of funerals, I've found that words can be so hard to come by at such times. Rock lyrics have filled the gap in so many instances, bridging the human and the divine.

Rockers realize that aging and even dying are a part of life. They sing sensitively and boldly of the truth as they experience it, a truth not unlike Ecclesiastes' acknowledgement that there is "a season" for everything and "a time for every purpose under heaven." Rock artists sing with sadness at all that we lose in and through the aging process. Yet these prophets of rock also sing with hope, hope for a joyous journey, hope for a love that endures, and hope in an eternal life, an enduring connection with those who matter most to us in this life. The hope rockers offer is not unlike the hope of which Jesus spoke toward the end of his life, when he said to his beloved disciples, "Let not your hearts be troubled. Neither let them be afraid," and "remember, I am with you always, even to the end of the age."(John 14:1, Matthew 28:)

Resurrection

"Yesterday I would not have believed that
tomorrow the sun would shine
Then one day you came into my life. I am alive again!
"Alive Again" – Chicago

At the center of the Christian faith stands
the almost unfathomable notion of resurrection, the claim that Jesus
of Nazareth, having died the cruelest of deaths, came out of the grave,
alive. More astonishing still is Christianity's contention that one day
we, too, will rise from the dead, just as Jesus did. The Apostle Paul
highlighted the importance of this belief in Jesus' resurrection in the
following way: "If Christ hasn't raised from the dead, your faith is
futile...If only for this life we have hope in Christ, we are to be pitied
more than all men." (I Corinthians 15:17,19) But just as Paul recognized the central importance of the resurrection to Christian faith,
he also acknowledged how tough it is to believe in it. Paul referred
to Christ's rising from the dead as "a stumbling block to the Jews and
foolishness to the Gentiles."(I Corinthians 1:23) If it was a major

stumbling block for people back in the first century, the resurrection is that much harder to swallow for people in the 21st century.

It's understandable that we should find resurrection hard, if not impossible, to believe. On the other hand, there is so much here on earth that cries out that death is not the last word. The natural realm is filled with resurrections. Every sunset brings a darkness that seems both impenetrable and permanent. Yet each morning's sunrise brings light and life to all things. Each Fall a dying process begins that affects all plant life, from the tiniest flower to the largest tree. Leaves and petals are ripped from their life source and left scattered on the soon-to-be frozen ground. Winter's deep freeze then pounds what seems to be the final nail in the coffin of all that was once so brilliantly alive. And yet, somehow, Spring miraculously awakens all that seemed dead for months. The trees bud; the flowers blossom; the leaves return. Resurrection is strangely both contrary to natural law and completely in line with it.

Jesus, himself, seemed to suggest that dying is actually a prerequisite for true, full life to emerge when he said, "Unless a kernel of wheat falls into the ground and dies, it remains only a single seed. But if it dies, it produces many seeds." (John 12:24) Elsewhere Jesus says, "Whoever finds his life will lose it, whoever loses his life for my sake will find it." (Matthew 10:39) Many of us have heard story upon story from those who have been pronounced dead later reawakening with descriptions of bright lights, audible voices, and a peace beyond all measure. A young man in my church recently sat with his dying dad, holding his hand as his father breathed his last. The surviving son called me right after his father passed and said, "It was an incredible moment! I saw light all around him, and it was like his spirit just rose and left his body."

Rock-n-roll artists have been singing about life after death and newness of life in the here and now for decades, sometimes metaphorically, and at other times quite literally. Norman Greenbaum's "Spirit in the Sky" came out in 1969 and refuses to go away. Just a few days ago, I heard it on a television commercial for a product I can't even remember. Greenbaum affirms that when we die, we go "up to the Spirit in the sky," to the place "that's the best."

George Harrison's best-known contribution to The Beatles' cata-
logue, "Here Comes the Sun," has new life at its center. The sun comes
up after a "long, cold, lonely winter," and it causes smiles to "return
to the faces." The repetition of "Here comes the sun," along with the
tag line, "it's alright," offers hope and assurance for newness of life.

In the mid-70s, the ground-breaking, jazz-rock band, Chicago, bore
witness to such new life in their upbeat anthem "Alive Again." Like
Adam and Eve in the garden on the second day of creation, Chicago
sings, "Yesterday I would not have believed that tomorrow the sun
would shine." Then an unnamed "you" enters the scene, inspiring
the singer to cry out, "I am alive again!" As the song continues and
the singer receives the love of the mysterious other, he finds that his
life completely changes, and the only words he can come up with to
express the overwhelming and positive change in him are those of
resurrection: "new life," "sunshine," and feeling "alive again."

In her second album, released in 1995, Tracy Chapman sang of
resurrection as well. She looked at the broken world all around her
and wondered if it was even "worth fixing." (Tracy Chapman, "New
Beginning") The sheer volume of "pain and suffering" Chapman
observed and experienced all around her warranted "starting all over."
She assures us that she loves life; it's just that she's reached a tipping
point of sorts. The haunting moan of a didgeridoo, woven through
the song's background, emphasizes the desperation Chapman feels.
The world about which Tracy sings is messed up, but amidst its brokenness and fragmentation, Chapman remains hopeful that we really
can "make new symbols" and "start all over."

Chapman's sense of urgency and desperation about the direction
of our world proved prophetic when the events of 9/11 occurred.
The brokenness of humanity, the pain and suffering inflicted, both
in the attacks themselves and in the subsequent retaliatory war and
occupation, gave flesh to Chapman's call for new language and a
new start.

Spiritual rocker, Bruce Springsteen, dedicated an entire album to
9/11 and called it, interestingly enough, *The Rising*. The title cut from
this 2002 release tells the story of a New York City fireman rushing up

into one of the towers with a half-mile of line and an oxygen tank on his back. He wears "the cross of his calling," and goes into the very tower from which everyone else is fleeing. Springsteen ends "The Rising" with a vision of sorts. He imagines the ascending fireman looking down at his wife in a garden, where she is holding pictures of their children, as the sky above her turns black. In this dream-like state, we can almost hear the ascending fireman calling out to his loved ones below, "Come on up for the rising." In that fireman's call to his envisioned family, he assures them that the very place to which he is rising is the one to which they too will rise one day. It's almost as if in climbing that soon-to-crumble tower, the fireman not only ensured his own death, but simultaneously began his ascent to life anew, to resurrection. In this heroic scene, Springsteen's listener can't help but hear echoes of Jesus' notion that "if anyone loses his life for my sake, he will surely find it." (Matthew 10:39)

Los Lonely Boys offer a more escapist interpretation of the afterlife in their 2004 hit, "Heaven." Like Chapman, this band struggles with the present world situation, opening with "Save me from this prison! Lord, help me get away!" They want out of their current "misery," weariness, and craziness. Their repeated chorus, "How far is heaven?" indicates that they understand resurrection as an escape from this world and the fulfillment of a universal longing for a place of peace.

Yusuf Islam, the artist formerly known as Cat Stevens, released his first record in over 25 years in 2006, a musical resurrection if there ever was one. Now a strict Muslim, Yusuf dreams of a place he's "still to find," where "a new life" awaits. His vision of heaven, or perhaps an age to come, is an "open world, borderless and wide," "where...nobody's taking sides." ("Maybe There's a World," Yusuf Islam, 2006)

My own struggles believing in the resurrection lessened once my mother passed away. Since her sudden and unexpected death, my siblings and I have all had inexplicable experiences of mom's continued presence. My eldest brother felt her hand gently patting his head, as he lay in bed grieving her loss one night. In the middle of mom's memorial service, I was overcome with an impulse to get out of my seat and go to the back of the church, where a couple was sitting by themselves, respectfully distant from our family. I ushered them forward, inviting them to huddle with the rest of us. Those who know me were shocked by this gesture, while those who knew my mother saw my action as completely consistent with what she'd have done in this particular situation. I described the experience later, saying, "I felt like I was being led through the entire thing." It was the first — but not the last — experience I've had of mom's living, resurrected presence.

I am a notoriously impatient person. I despise lines and those whose actions prolong my wait. Two months after my mother's passing, I was caught in the "12 items or less" aisle at the grocery store. There was a lady two spots ahead of me who had at least 20 items in her overflowing basket, and the incompetent cashier-in-training couldn't have been any slower. I felt my blood pressure rise, my teeth clench, and my mind conjuring hell-fire for those ahead of me. Then, suddenly, I heard my mother's voice. I actually heard her whispering, clearly and naturally, "Now, Toby, relax. This isn't a big deal. Take a deep breath." A part of me wanted to tell mom to "shut up," which is exactly what I often did when she offered me such unsolicited, pollyannish advice throughout her life. Like the compulsion to leave my seat at the funeral two months before, however, I knew this wise plea for patience was coming from somewhere outside of me. I knew it was my mother's voice and her heart at work. She was alive. She had risen.

Six and a half years have passed since mom was killed, and I've felt her presence more palpably since her death than I ever did when she was alive. As a pastor, I've lost count of the number of men, women, and children who have been in my office trying to make sense of similar experiences with their deceased love ones. I try to affirm the reality and authenticity of what they're experiencing, often pointing them to the natural world, where resurrection is woven into the very fabric of each and every day. I've also been known to give my grieving parishioners a list of some of my favorite resurrection rock songs to listen to, just so they'll know that they're in good company.

In the end, none of us can prove that there is life after death or that resurrection is real. Still, no one can disprove it either. Jesus did his level best to assure us that death did not and would not have the last word. In John 14, he asks his followers not to be afraid, but to believe in him. "In my Father's house are many rooms...and I am going to prepare a place for you, that one day, where I am you may be also." (John 14:2-3)

Even I — a minister — have doubts about life after death from time to time. Still, thanks to my mom, my church family, and the testimony of some of my favorite rock songs, my belief in the promised resurrection usually wins out. "Lord, I believe; help my unbelief." (Mark 9:24)

In Search of Fulfillment

"You can't always get what you want."
— The Rolling Stones

"I still haven't found what I'm looking for."
— U2

A middle-aged woman walked into her therapist's office and said, "I should be happy with the way things are. I have a fine marriage, two wonderful kids, and a good career. Yet I keep feeling something is missing... Deep down I am restless. I want something more..." (Gerald May, "Entering the Emptiness" in *Simple Living, Compassionate Life*, Living the Good News, 1999, p. 46)

"It seems to me some fine things have been laid upon your table,
but you only want the ones that you can't get."
— The Eagles

A young man spends more and more time surfing the net, looking for free pornography sites. There's something thrilling about his covert search, as he draws nearer to the forbidden fruit of erotic photos, with his kids asleep in the next room, and his wife upstairs. What he finds excites his eyes, and from there his imagination takes over, but the thrill is gone even before he shuts down his computer. Then the inevitable self-loathing begins.

> *"I can't get no satisfaction. But I try and I try and I try…"*
> – The Rolling Stones

There is, in all of us, a chronic restlessness, a longing, a hunger, a seeking for that which we can't even name, that which is always just beyond our reach. Rockers from Mick Jagger and The Stones all the way to Bono and U2 have sung passionately of the human inability to achieve fulfillment in this life. The giants of the literary world have affirmed this very same thing. Take a look at Dean Moriarity in Kerouac's *On the Road* or at any of the characters in Fitzgerald's *The Great Gatsby*, and you'll see eternally restless hearts involved in a frenzied search for fulfillment that is ultimately fruitless. Even the 'real life' celebrities who seem to have it all — wealth, friends, lovers, status, power, and freedom — find that fulfillment is forever just out of reach. Bruce Springsteen was right when he sang, "Everybody's got a hungry heart," (Bruce Springsteen, "Hungry Heart")

But of all the literary and musical treatments of man's quest for fulfillment, it is U2's hit single "I Still Haven't Found What I'm Looking For" that offers the most powerful and authentic treatment of this universal theme. Its first verse speaks of the physical realm where the singer has climbed mountains, run through fields, and scaled "city walls," but, "still hasn't found what he's looking for." In the second verse, the singer turns to the sexual realm, kissing, being touched, and experiencing "burning desire." But he still hasn't found what he's looking for. In the final verse, Bono moves to the spiritual realm, speaking with "eternal angels," holding "hands with the Devil." He then makes explicit reference to his Christian faith: Jesus breaking "the bonds" and loosing "the chains," even carrying "the cross." Bono goes on to emphasize the fervency of his Christian faith, crying, "You know I believe it!" But ultimately U2 does what no one else has had the guts to do. They admit that even with their Christian faith in tact, they "still haven't found what (they're) looking for." In unprecedented fashion, Bono confesses that even with faith, even with the assurance of Christ's redeeming, atoning work on the cross, he and his mates still haven't found what they're looking for.

After studying the lyrics of this amazing song, I eventually realized how radical its message is, especially given that it was written and sung by the one person in my lifetime who epitomizes authentic Christian faith. From this realization, it didn't take long for my heart and head to figure out that what I was hearing, at long last, was the Truth — with a capital T. Human fulfillment or self-actualization in this life, with or without Christian faith, is a myth. A hungry heart, an insatiable appetite, an inability to achieve satisfaction is part of what makes us human. Restlessness and a measure of discontent are enduring realities that even faith cannot take away.

U2's authenticity in exposing the lie behind the damaging myth of fulfillment set me free to explore the positives of my own enduring emptiness. Finally, I could stop wasting so much time and energy looking for something I would never find. As Gerald May writes,

> "We make several great mistakes if we think life should or even can be resolved to a point of complete serenity and fulfillment. To believe this is to commit ourselves to a fantasy that does not exist, and that, if it were true, would kill our love and end in stagnation, boredom, and death...Most importantly, the myth of fulfillment makes us miss the most beautiful aspect of our human souls: our emptiness, our incompleteness, our radical yearning for love. We were never meant to be completely fulfilled; we were meant to taste it, to long for it, to grow toward it...To miss our emptiness is, finally, to miss our hope."
>
> (Gerald May, "Entering the Emptiness," in *Simple Living, Compassionate Life*, Living the Good News, 1999, p. 47)

Gerald May is right. In all of my professional and personal study of the Old and New Testaments, I have never found any reason to believe that God's goal for me or for any of us is that we be happy or fulfilled. The abundant life Jesus spoke of is not to be confused with the materially minded American dream, nor with some self-centered state called happiness. To buy into that corrupt gospel of prosperity requires confusing our society's ideal of the good life with the Biblical notion of abundant life. What Jesus spoke of was a life lived in partnership with our Creator. "Emmanuel" — God coming to be with us — is the ultimate message of Christianity. God's message has never been 'Let me make your life wonderful, happy, and trouble free.' That's the lie, the cultural myth. It's the sales pitch believers throw at those they hope will join their ranks.

Deep down, we all know the truth, don't we? Committed people of faith are not any more satisfied or fulfilled than those who make no faith claims. We who believe still haven't found what we're looking for.

In the end, the promise of the Christian faith is this and only this: God cares for and loves us enough to come join us in our emptiness, to enter our brokenness, and to be with us in our longing. It has been honest rock-n-rollers who have taught me God is not necessarily going to cure our cancer, fix our bad marriages, or make us happy throughout our lives. God is not even going to fill that hole the each of us has inside — not completely, not yet.

Why not? Why hasn't Bono, who sits at the very pinnacle of rock stardom and Christian faith, found what he's looking for? The twelfth chapter of Paul's letter to the Romans provides a possible explanation. Paul compares the human family to a human body and writes, "when one part suffers all parts suffer with it." (Romans 12:26) Perhaps happiness, fulfillment, and contentment escape us and will continue to do so until all God's children are cared for. If we are all brothers and sisters, all members of God's family, if the ties that bind the entire creation together are God-ordained, why should any of us expect to be happy when nearly two thirds of the world lives in extreme poverty? Should any of us expect to be fulfilled and content when American children under the age of 13 have more spending money — $230 per year — than the 300 million poorest people in the world earn in a year? (Alan Durning, "How much is enough?" in Simple Living, Compassionate Life, pgs. 90–91) At my graduation from Princeton Seminary in 1987, the great Frederich Buechner challenged us, saying that there would never be peace and joy for any of us until there is peace and joy for all of us.

Phillip Gulley and James Mulholland wrestle with this tension throughout their amazing book *If Grace Is True*. As they discuss the parable of the wedding banquet from Matthew 22, they focus on the host being so troubled by all the empty seats at the table that he sends his servants out into the streets to bring in everybody they find. Gulley and Mulholland then endorse the interpretation of Methodist theologian David Lowes Watson:

> "There are still too many empty places at the banquet table. The appropriate attitude for guests who have already arrived, therefore, is to nibble at the appetizers, and anticipate the feast to come. To sit down and begin to eat would be an unpardonable lapse of good manners, especially since the host is out looking for the missing guests and could certainly use some help."
> (Gulley & Mulholland, *If Grace is True*, Harper Collins, 2003, p. 189)

Maybe our ultimate contentment and lasting personal fulfillment are not meant to arrive until God's kingdom comes and God's will is done on earth as it is in heaven? Maybe we still haven't found what we're looking for because the God we worship still hasn't found what He's looking for.

Many Roads and Other Sheep

"We're one, but we're not the same,
we get to carry each other"
"One" – U2

One of the great dividers in theology today is the question of who is in and who is out, who is going to heaven and who is going the other way. I had lunch today with an 83 year-old woman who can't bring herself to join our church, because to do so she would be required to say that "Jesus is Lord." If she were to say that, she believes that she'd be condemning three-fourths of the world.

In the third book of his *A New Kind of Christian* trilogy, Brian McLaren tells a similar story. In the opening pages, his pastor/narrator has a conversation with his daughter when she returns home from college. She confesses to her pastor father that she can no longer embrace Christianity.

> "Daddy, if God is going to send all my friends to hell, then he can send me right along with them, because I love them, and I'd rather be loyal to them than save my own skin…The little I know about Jesus — I don't think

he would want to sit up in the living room, having a big party with his Father and all his friends, while some of his other friends are frying in the basement. Everything I know about Jesus tells me he would go down there and get them out."

(Brian McLaren, The Last Word and the Word After That, Jossy-Bass, 2005, pgs. 30, 32)

Mainline denominations, including my own (PCUSA), have been too preoccupied over questions like whether homosexuals should be allowed to serve in positions of leadership to take on McLaren's much more essential question. It won't be long, however, before all denominations will be forced to wrestle with the question of universal salvation. In the meantime, we misguided Christians will continue to divide ourselves over less eternal controversies, as we saw during the presidential race of 2004, when a pastor in North Carolina declared that anyone voting for Democrat John Kerry would no longer be welcome in his church.

Intra-religious splintering is nothing new. Through the centuries, religious folks have divided themselves into factions, drawn battle line after battle line, and created more divisions than the Chinese army. Jesus consistently operated from a posture of radical grace, accepting and embracing even those whom religious leaders of his day had condemned. Many of Christ's followers in today's Christian churches, however, are more apt to be exclusivist and quick to judge others as unworthy and unwelcome in God's kingdom.

Rock-n-rollers have often been more Christ-like and grace-filled than many self-proclaimed Christians when it comes to their assessment of who will be in God's kingdom and who won't. In "The Sea Refuses No river," Pete Townsend uses the poetry of nature to remind us of God's gracious, inclusive tendencies. "…we're polluted now, but, in our hearts, still clean…Whether stinking and rank or red from the tank, the sea refuses no river." While Townsend echoes Paul's declaration of universal human sin from Romans 3, he does so with a strong undercurrent of grace. No river is refused by Townsend's all-welcoming sea.

Stevie Wonder's "Higher Ground," more recently covered by the Red Hot Chile Peppers, is an encouraging call to all people to reach for "higher ground." He acknowledges many pathways to the divine kingdom. Whether we're teachers, preachers, or soldiers, it is by passionately applying ourselves to our work, by being our best selves, that we climb Stevie Wonder's stairway to heaven. His stairway, like Townsend's sea, is open and available to all.

U2's "One" offers this same inclusive truth, albeit more subtly. While we're "one," we're "not the same." We need to "carry each other, carry each other." "One" is no romantic love song (despite the fact that many couples play it at their weddings). U2 challenges us all to love and care for others, especially those who have hurt us and those whom we have hurt: "We hurt each other then we do it again." Jesus made the same point when he said, "If you love those who love you, what reward will you get? Are not even the tax collectors doing that?...But I tell you: love your enemies and pray for those who persecute you." (Matthew 5:44, 46) U2 further reveals their connection to Christ's all-inclusive, no boundaries love in "City of Blinding Lights," which ends with the grace-filled truth that, "blessings are not just for the ones who kneel, luckily."

"Black and White," the Three-Dog Night hit of the early 70s, is another of rock's odes to inclusiveness that mirrors Christ-like grace. This David Arkin composition begins with a clear acknowledgment of the differences in humanity — black and white, day and night. The song ultimately affirms that it's only "together" that we learn and "see the light." Likewise, The Youngbloods recognized that humanity's true potential depended on our getting together, with their famous words, "C'mon people... everybody get together, try to love one another right now." (The Youngbloods, "Get Together")

Jamaican reggae master Bob Marley, also an intensely spiritual rocker, saw the strength and power of humanity as lying in our underlying oneness, our ability to come together. "One love, one heart, let's get together and be alright." Marley believed that we were one family under God, meant to "give thanks and praise to the Lord and be alright." (Bob Marley, "One Love")

Rock's celebration of underlying unity amidst our external differences continued (albeit in an admittedly cheesy fashion) when Paul McCartney and Stevie Wonder got together in the 1980s to record

"Ebony and Ivory." Using the black and white piano keys as a metaphor for racial and other human differences, these two rock icons exemplified the "perfect harmony" of which we all are capable. They affirmed, despite any and all differences, that "people are the same wherever you go." Our task is to "learn to give each other what we need to survive, together alive."

While so many rockers have demonstrated the ability to celebrate diversity and, at the same time, affirm our fundamental oneness as humans, religions in general — and Christianity in particular — have for centuries focused on differences, building far more walls than bridges. The history of the Christian church is filled with schism after schism. There are literally hundreds of Christian denominations in America alone, a testament to our obsession with differences and our refusal to define ourselves according to what we share.

It's important, however, that we not equate what the Christian church has done with what its Founder intended. I am not the only pastor who believes we Christians have completely misrepresented Jesus and his Word by focusing so resolutely on who is in and who is out, who is saved and who isn't. Was the Jesus of the Gospels really a divider, obsessed with human and religious differences? Did Jesus focus more on what separated people than on what united them?

Even a cursory run through the gospels reveals an undeniable, definitive picture of a Christ who was far more inclusive than exclusive. It reveals a Christ far more interested in bridge building than in erecting walls. In Matthew 5:43-47, Jesus taught that, in God's design, the sun and rain fall equally "on the just and the unjust," and that we were to "love our enemies." Those are hardly the words of a divider. In the famous sheep and goats passage from Matthew 25:31ff, Jesus is clear that he expects his followers to feed, clothe, visit, house, and welcome all people indiscriminately, even and especially "the least of these." While some Christians believe Matthew 25 to be a judgment on non-believers or those of other religions, the text itself simply doesn't allow for such an interpretation. His intent in this pivotal parable is to emphasize the inextricable link that ties all human brothers and sisters together as children of God. Those welcomed by Christ in Matthew 25 were not expecting to be ushered into his kingdom. They hadn't recognized that when they had served the least among humans, they'd actually been serving Jesus. The ones Jesus ended up banishing, on the other hand, thought they were "in" and on the same side as Jesus. The truth of the sheep and goats parable boils down to this: to be a follower of Christ requires that we never pass by a fellow human who is in need, for we all are God's children.

Even John's gospel, generally thought of as more divisive and dualistic than the synoptics, manages to convey God's all-inclusive, universal love. John calls Jesus "the good shepherd," who knows his sheep by name and cares for them passionately, even at great risk to himself. John's Jesus goes on to call himself the "gate for the sheep," through which one must enter to be saved. (John 10:9) While this sounds extremely exclusive on its own, Christians have repeatedly failed to notice that only seven verses later, still in John 10, Jesus adds, "And I have other sheep that are not of this fold. I must bring them in also." (John 10:16) How revealing that one of the most inclusive statements Jesus ever uttered in John 10:16 is so consistently ignored by his followers in favor of what he said a mere seven verses earlier. It is as though the exclusivists want no part of the wider gate that Jesus himself opened.

As we move out of the gospels into The Acts of the Apostles, even Peter, who had previously revealed his own closed-minded exclusiveness from time to time, ended up with a very inclusive notion of God's kingdom and Christ's 'for everybody' grace. After having a vision on a rooftop, Peter travels willingly with a Gentile, goes into another Gentile's house, and eats Gentile (unkosher) food there. These were all blatant violations of Jewish law. Peter follows up these highly unusual and unprecedented actions with an amazing and utterly bridge-building speech.

> "You are well aware that it is against our law for a Jew to associate with Gentiles or visit them. But God has shown me that I should not call anyone impure or unclean…I now realize how true it is that God does not show favoritism but accepts those from every nation who revere Him and do what is right."
>
> (Acts 10:28-35)

Late in his life, Peter finally captures the essential core of Jesus' message: grace for all people, for all of creation. This very message, however, has been not only missed, but corrupted by many of today's Christians.

I began my own Christian pilgrimage as a Pharisaic follower, convinced of my own right-ness and righteousness. Militant in my evangelicalism, I firmly believed the rest of the world (defined as all those who did not believe exactly what and how I believed) was wrong and on the highway to hell. It was the job of 'true Christians' like me to save 'them' before it was too late. I remember going door to door in my fraternity house to my totally uninterested and freaked-out fraternity brothers, with tracts explaining the "Four Spiritual Laws." I even visited some of my professors and sketched out for them the infamous bridge diagram, showing the huge chasm that separated them from God, a chasm of sin that only Jesus could bridge on the cross. I was a Zealot for Christ, willing to sacrifice popularity for spiritual brownie points. I even tried to convert the women I dated, often giving them the ultimatum: either they 'accept Christ,' or accept that we would no longer be a couple. Only years later did I realize the one HUGE problem with what I was doing: the Jesus I wanted others to 'accept' bore little resemblance to the Jesus of scripture.

Jesus spent his entire life trying to move humans beyond the 'Us vs. Them' paradigm. At every turn, he put himself in close relationships with society's 'them.' The only group that Jesus consistently condemned and castigated was the religious leaders — the ultimate exclusivists — the ones who assumed they were right and everyone else was wrong. (Sounds a little like me in college.) Jesus loved, accepted, and served prostitutes, the demon-possessed, tax collectors, extortionists, notorious sinners, and betrayers. He reserved his hammer of justice for those who felt they had a monopoly on religious truth. "Not everyone who says to me, 'Lord, Lord,' will enter the kingdom of heaven, but only those who do the will of my Father..." (Matthew 7:21) Earlier in the same chapter, Jesus says, "Do not judge, lest you also be judged. For in the same way you judge others, you will be judged." (Matthew 7:1-2) It is difficult, if not impossible, to reconcile these clear, inclusive teachings of Jesus with the exclusivist, wall-building interpretations and endeavors of so many of his modern-day followers. It is far easier to find the grace-based spirit of Christ in the best rock songs of the last 50 years.

Artists throughout the five-decade history of rock-n-roll have repeatedly emphasized the oneness of all creation lying beneath our wonderful diversity. They've also celebrated the equality of all people and affirmed the need for us to come together. Rockers have correctly tied our incredible potential for good to our willingness to set aside our differences. In doing these things, rockers have often brought their listeners closer to the true perspective of Jesus than I ever did in college and closer than many Christian leaders have over the last five decades.

On the heels of rock's prophets has come a new breed of theologians with the potential to set Christians straight on the inclusive nature of God's kingdom. These compassionate, post-modern, post-Christian, thoughtful, and thoroughly biblical thinkers — Rob Bell, Brian McLaren, Donald Miller, Phillip Gulley, James Mulholland, and others — are worth listening to. So, too, are the thoughtful rock artists, who have been unintentionally closer to Christ than they or we ever imagined. Perhaps this new breed of theologians may, at long last, join forces with rock-n-roll singers, leading the rest of us back to a more harmonious relationship with all of creation and with God, who is always a builder of bridges and a destroyer of walls.

The sooner we figure out that there are many roads to Truth and to God, the sooner we will live into our amazing potential as humans. Our potential — and, at this point, our very survival — is dependent upon our coming together as fellow children of God, despite any and all differences. Prophetic rockers have been calling us to such radical unity for more than 50 years. Jesus, with both his words and his grace-filled life, has been calling us to be "one" for nearly 2000 years! (John 17:20-21)

Compassion

"God forbid you ever have to walk a mile
in her shoes, 'cause then you really might
know what it's like to sing the blues"
"What It's Like" – Everlast

Michael was my small group Bible study leader in college. We also shared a house with a few other guys the year after I graduated. One night Michael asked me to take a walk, and I could tell he was deeply troubled. As we strolled the uneven sidewalks of Greencastle, Indiana, he shared his long-term, tenacious struggle to come to terms with his own sexuality. He said, "I'm afraid I might be gay...I don't want to be gay. I know it's wrong, and for the last few years I've prayed about it and fought my same-sex impulses with everything I've got. But it feels like it's just something I am, no matter how hard I try." He cried. I cried with him.

This was a first for me. I'd only known homosexuals from a distance. Growing up, I'd participated in all the locker room, gay-bashing jokes with my adolescent friends. I'd even developed a pretty tight biblical argument against homosexuality during my college years, but here I was, face to face with a gay friend, a fellow Christian, a spiritual mentor, a child of God with a huge and gracious heart.

We had been silent for several minutes as we walked, and I knew Michael was waiting anxiously for me to respond, to tell him what I thought. Everything that came into my head seemed lame and insensitive in the face of his genuine, real-life grief. Eventually, I just hugged him and thanked him for trusting me enough to share his burden. I told him I'd be there for him in whatever ways I could. I promised I'd pray with him and for him, and, though I wasn't in the habit of saying so to anyone back then, I told him I loved him, and I meant it.

Twenty-five years later, serving as a pastor in a church, I get asked all the time for my 'stand' on the 'issue' of homosexuality, and I think immediately of Michael. I don't see sexual orientation as an issue, nor do I see my role as taking a stand on other people's lives. It seems to me that our individual and collective stands or positions on these so-called issues are dividing us in extremely adversarial ways. Where we stand on homosexuality, abortion, immigration, the war in Iraq, world hunger, and poverty is ripping us apart: nation from nation, political party from political party, religion from religion, and even Christian brother from Christian sister. As our society grows more and more polarized every day, we are dividing ourselves — our families, our communities, our churches, our nations, and our world — over things that we really don't know a whole lot about. And the more stuck we become in our positions, the less able we are to be compassionate. That is what scares me most.

The word "compassion" comes from the prefix 'com' — meaning 'with' — and the root "passion" — meaning 'feel' or 'suffer.' According to Oregon State theologian, Marcus Borg, "compassion is the defining mark of the follower of Jesus." (Borg, *Meeting Jesus Again for the First Time*, Harper Collins, 1995, p. 136) As one seeking to follow Jesus, I can't overlook the clear pattern that whenever Jesus was put in a position where judgment was expected, he didn't deliver judgment; he delivered compassion instead. To the woman caught in the act of adultery, to a laborer who worked only the last hour of the day, to a corrupt tax collector named Zaccheus, to a prostitute who 'wasted' an expensive jar of perfume, to a disciple who swore never to deny him but then did three times, and to a common thief crucified on the cross next to him, to all these and to countless others, Jesus delivered compassion. The writer of Hebrews emphasizes Christ's unwavering commitment to feel with and suffer with us when he wrote: "For in Christ, we have not a high priest who is unable to sympathize with our weaknesses, but one who in every respect has been tempted as we have and has suffered as we suffer." (Hebrews 4:14-16)

That's why we need to listen to what some of the thoughtful, sensitive rock-n-roll artists have to say about compassion. For decades they have been reminding us of a vital spiritual truth: that until we walk a mile in someone else's shoes, we have no idea what that person's life is like, and, therefore, no right to judge him.

Everlast's smash hit, "What It's Like," is perhaps rock's most profound treatment of compassion. Their song tells the stories of three pitiable characters: a homeless beggar, a pregnant teen, and an armed drug dealer. After chronicling the horrors and inhumane treatment that each of these people endures, Everlast keeps coming back to the line "God forbid you ever had to walk a mile in his shoes, 'cause then you really might know what it's like to sing the blues."

The song's second verse focuses on a pregnant teen, and, in so doing, took me back to the late 70s, when the pastor of my family's church in Bay Village, Ohio said one of the most important things I've ever heard about abortion. He said, "You can say whatever you want about your stand on abortion. But until your 16 year-old daughter comes home pregnant, you don't really know where you stand." Our political and religious leaders are all-too-willing to spout off about their particular stands on this 'issue.'

Abortion isn't an issue, anymore than homosexuality is; abortion is people — real people with real feelings, real families, and, yes, even real faith! This was my pastor's point nearly 30 years ago. When we take stands on issues, we depersonalize and dehumanize our brothers and sisters who are involved in real life struggles.

As a pastor, it's sad for me to admit that in my experience, both in and out of the church, rock-n-rollers have been more compassionate in their treatment of these real people in their real life situations than religious and political leaders have. Think of Crash Test Dummies' "Mm-mm-mm" song, where they tell the story of a girl who wouldn't go into the locker room with the other girls until the teachers and administrators "finally made her." It was then that they found "birthmarks all over her body." Think of James Taylor's "Millworker," in which he tells the story of a woman whose drunken husband leaves her with "three faces to feed." So she goes to the mill where "it's me and my machine for the rest of the morning, the rest of the afternoon, and the rest of my life." Dozens of Bruce Springsteen's songs are written out of a profound compassion, and if we listen — really listen — to what he's saying, his songs evoke waves of compassion in us as well. "Born in the U.S.A." is an overwhelmingly compassionate look at a young man who "got in a hometown jam," and was sent to "go kill the yellow man." When this Vietnam veteran returns, he is an unwelcome stranger, even in his hometown. The local refinery won't hire him. Even the V.A. man assigned to his case offers him no help.

Like many of rock's greats, Springsteen's compassion runs much deeper than the lyrics he writes. I read once in *Rolling Stone* that the Boss shows up at his venues hours before the doors open. While his roadies are checking the sound, Springsteen moves from seat to seat. At each one he closes his eyes and imagines someone who might be sitting there when the show begins. He creates a likely scenario — a man whose wife has left him, or a single mom with two kids and a minimum wage job. He allows each scenario at each seat to sink into his head and heart. Then, when the curtain opens and the lights come up, Bruce sings to the people in those particular seats, filled with compassion for them, wanting to offer them some strength for their journeys.

I saw Bruce live for the first time in the mid 90s, when he was on his "The Ghost of Tom Joad" tour. It was just him on stage, all alone, with about a dozen black Takemine guitars, all the very same model that I played at the time. This was long before illegal immigration became the trendy topic that it is today. Bruce told and sang stories of compassion all night long, but they weren't his stories, exactly. They were stories told to him that he'd collected during the times he spent traveling incognito in border towns in Texas, Arizona, and California. He met immigrants — illegals — and sat in taverns with them, listening to their stories. Eventually, Bruce turned those immigrant stories into songs. The one I remember most was "Sinaloa Cowboys," the story of two brothers who risked everything to cross the Mexican/American border. Once they hit U.S. soil, they landed jobs as pickers but soon were asked by a stranger if they'd like to earn in a week what they'd been making per month. They knew something of the dangers inherent in Meth production, but the money was too good, and they had so much more to save if they were ever to bring their families over safely. So, they took the job making meth-amphetamines in a little shed. Faithfully saving all that they earned, the brothers buried their cash down by a little creek. One day, Miguel was outside the shed standing watch, "when the shack exploded." The song ends with the brutal image of Miguel carrying Luiz's body down to the creek side to bury him in the same hole in which they'd been stashing their money.

Sinaloa Cowboys is a compassionate portrayal of two brothers risking everything to chase a dream, the same dream that millions of others from lands far and wide have chased for nearly 300 years. Springsteen tells their tale in a way that makes us realize, when faced with what these brothers were in Mexico, along with the prospect of letting our families starve, we might have done the same thing.

I have to believe that the compassion of rock musicians like Springsteen, James Taylor, Everlast, Crash Test Dummies, and many others has something to do with why today's kids and young adults spend so little time in church and so much time and money listening to and downloading rock-n-roll music. When was the last time you heard a pastor, imam, or rabbi talk about abortion even half as sensitively as Ben Folds does in "Brick?" Folds deals with this story — his own true story, by the way — in the first person. He, himself, is the boyfriend who got his girlfriend pregnant. He, himself, drives his lover to the clinic, waits outside, buys her flowers, and later endures the long, silent ride home, where, though the two are in the same car, "she's alone and I'm alone, now I know it." Folds, like so many of his fellow rockers, doesn't waste his time (nor ours) articulating his stand on abortion. He and his girlfriend don't have that luxury; they're already in the thick of the situation, and the situation couldn't be more real or more gut-wrenching. Folds simply tells the story, as if to say, 'this is how it was for my girlfriend and me.' There's no preaching or moralizing; there is no stand-taking. There is only Folds' compassion and his hope that his listeners might learn to be a little more compassionate as well.

As a pastor, I still get asked all the time for my "stands" on a wide range of issues. I used to get sucked into these inevitable and un-winable debates, but thanks to rock-n-roll music, I take an entirely different approach now. I respond to my inquisitor with a gentle reminder that we're talking about people and not issues. Then I do what rock-n-roll singers have been doing for years; I tell stories, stories that are personal, real, and true. This is the most compassionate approach I've ever come across, and it's one I learned from my favorite rock musicians and bands, not from the church.

Thanks to rockers like Ben Folds, Everlast, Bruce Springsteen, and others, I've come to see that no matter what the 'topic' or 'issue,' compassion is the best starting point. It allows us to affirm our fundamental oneness as humans before we even discuss our differences. In Christ, God came to feel with us, to suffer with us, and, in a sense, to walk in our shoes. At the very core of Christianity is the power of compassion to unify, to draw together, to personalize, to build bridges, and to tear down walls. It saddens me when the great power of Christ's compassion is replaced with judgment, a judgment used to divide, to separate, to generalize, to dismiss, or even to condemn those in whose shoes we've yet to walk.

What I hear at the core of so many great rock-n-roll songs is the same unequivocal call I hear in the gospels: for the people of this world to be more concerned with being compassionate than with being right.

Conclusion

In his seminal work of 1951, *Christ & Culture*, H. Richard Niebuhr argued that there are five ways of understanding the complex relationship between Jesus of Nazareth and the culture of his day. The first of these Christ/culture relationships that Niebuhr explored is "Christ *against* culture." In this view, Christians "reject all of cultural society; a clear line of separation is drawn between the brotherhood of the children of God and the world." (H. Richard Niebuhr, *Christ & Culture*, Harper Collins, 1951, pgs. 47–8) Niebuhr goes on to argue that in this particular understanding of Christ, "the world appears as a realm under the power of evil; it is the region of darkness, into which the citizens of the kingdom of light must not enter." (p. 48) It is crucial to point out that Niebuhr did not endorse the Christ against culture view, but simply sought to emphasize its subtle yet strong hold on so many Christians in his day.

Contemporary theologian Brian McLaren doesn't endorse the Christ vs. culture paradigm either; in fact, he lambastes it. After lamenting that it is "too often practiced in the modern world," McLaren continues with tremendous sarcasm, saying,

> "It's okay to withdraw all our energies from the arts and culture 'out there' as long as we have a good choir and nice sanctuary 'in here.' It's okay because, after all, we're

about salvaging individuals from a sinking ship; neighbor-
hoods, economies, cultures, and all but individual human
souls will sink, so who cares?
(Brian McLaren, *Church on the Other Side*,
Zondervan Press, 1998, p. 42)

With this fear-based, closed-minded "Christ against culture"
paradigm holding sway with so many American Christians, it's no
wonder rock-n-roll music has been such a convenient whipping boy
for anti-culture Christians. All things rock have been lumped together
with drugs, profanity, pornography, and all the other products of the
dark side — products which, religious zealots believe, have been
specifically designed to lead our children astray and to increase the
Devil's dominion.

Thanks to this fear-driven and reactionary perspective — one that
takes only one-fifth of Niebuhr's analysis into account — many well-
intentioned Christians have tended to dismiss rock music without ever
giving it a chance. Admittedly, there is plenty of rock that deserves
to be dismissed out-of-hand. Still, so much of the best of rock-n-roll
music is deeply and inherently spiritual, profoundly positive, and
surprisingly in line with the teachings of Jesus.

By dismissing all rock-n-roll as evil, so many Christians and churches
have also inadvertently dismissed a huge number of people for whom
rock has sacred, spiritual status. Just as importantly, those who 'dis'
rock have limited the power of the God they claim is omnipotent.
Most tragic and significant of all, rock fearing, anti-culture Christians
have missed the very point of the incarnation of God in Christ. Robert
Webber put it this way:

> "What the Incarnation means for the arts is that the
> divine chooses to become present through creation,
> through wood, stone, mortar, color, sound, shape, form,
> movement, and action. Christians are not Gnostics. We
> do not reject the body, the material, the tangible. To do
> so would be to reject the Incarnation."
> (Robert Webber, *Signs of Wonder*, p. 87–88,
> quoted by Brian McLaren, *Church on the Other Side*,
> Zondervan Press, 1998, p. 67)

It is time we Christians stop operating exclusively out of a one-fifth understanding of H. Richard Niebuhr's analysis of Christ's relationship to his culture. Niebuhr did offer four other ways to understand Christ's relationship to the contemporary culture, including Christ *in* culture and Christ *transforming culture*. It is time that we let go of the narrowly defined, fear based, and anti-culture Christ, and re-examine the Christ who entered fully *into* the culture of his day. As we take this reconciling step, we will find ourselves much more able to respectfully engage the contemporary culture, understanding its artistic expressions as potential playgrounds of the Spirit. We will, in fact, be able to see and experience God and His work everywhere.

On the other hand, if we continue to draw artificial boundaries around what God can and can't do, where God can and can't be present, we will only be hastening our own demise by becoming modern-day Pharisees.

Rock-n-roll music represents a potential bridge between those currently inside the church and those outside it. By entering into the canon of rock-n-roll lyrics with a genuine openness to the "new wine" God has for us there, we can take an important and respectful first step toward the very people we have alienated over the course of the last sixty years. Rather than lambasting what is unsavory or even despicable in the worst of rock-n-roll, it's time to lift up and celebrate the spiritual themes we find in the best of rock music.

For me, it has been helpful to view rock-n-roll musicians within the larger Judeo-Christian tradition of the prophets. Prophets from Jeremiah and Isaiah all the way to John the Baptist, have all been unattractive and even threatening characters to the religious establishment of their day. From their clothing and hair on down to their unusual eating habits and inflammatory vocabulary, prophets have always been both hard to listen to and easy to dismiss. Nevertheless, God has consistently chosen such unsavory outsiders to bring His corrective, reforming message to the more polished community of religious insiders. By no means would anyone who listens carefully to rock music ever seek to elevate all or even a majority of rockers to the status of prophet. At the same time, though, we'd better be very careful about hastily dismissing all rock-n-rollers, as if none could be God's modern-day mouthpiece.

The time has come for religious people in general and Christians in particular to take the advice that Bob Dylan offered 50 years ago — to stop criticizing what we don't even understand. ("The Times They are a'changin") Whether it's female preachers, freed slaves, homosexuals, evolutionists, kids covered in tattoos and body piercings, people of other religions, or rock-n roll musicians, we who claim to follow Christ can no longer allow our lack of understanding to produce fear, judgment, religious arrogance, and further closed-mindedness.

Rob Bell, postmodern theologian and founding pastor of the enormous Mars Hill Community, recently filled large venues all across the country with a simple, appealing message — "Everything is spiritual." The inviting openness of Bell's tour title and talk proved to be both refreshing and edifying to the hundreds of thousands of spiritual seekers in this country, whose thirst for God has never been quenched by the narrow, tepid waters of traditional religion.

So much of the language in traditional Christian doctrine gives God credit for creating all that is. Christians claim to believe God inspired the scriptures and established His church. The Nicene Creed states that God made the heavens and the earth and all that is within them and that "without Him nothing was made that was made." The scriptures themselves say that God is Spirit and that God is everywhere in nature. Christian hymns and worship services "crown Him with many crowns" and call Him "Lord of all" — ALL things! (Or is that all things except rock-n-roll?)

Rock music is a spiritual well of tremendous depth. By declaring it unfit to drink, too many churches and Christians have essentially dismissed the dominant, most influential cultural expression of the last sixty years. When we Christians 'dis' rock-n-roll and repeatedly warn Christ's followers of its dangers, we might as well hang a huge sign at the front door of our churches that says, "We are irrelevant. Don't bother."

It would be ludicrous to suggest that the mass exodus of young people from the church in the last forty years was caused by its wholesale rejection of rock music. It is not so outlandish, however, to posit that the Church's often arrogant and dismissive attitude toward rock and other legitimate cultural and spiritual expressions is a telling symptom of a much larger disease that the younger generations clearly have no interest in contracting.

If you want to build a bridge between yourself and a teenager or young adult, ask her what kind of music she likes and who her favorite bands are. If you want that bridge to last, ask her if you could borrow and listen to a couple of her favorite CDs. If you can't make out the lyrics as you listen, go on-line and Google the song title. You'll be directed to dozens of free sites that offer the full, printable lyrics to just about any song. Listen to the song a few times with the lyrics in front of you and follow along. Have a follow up conversation as you return the discs. Show your young friend the lyric sheets you tracked down — she'll be impressed — and ask her to go over them with you and show you what they say to her. You might also bring some of the lyrics of the songs examined in this book. (See Appendix) As you open yourselves, together, to rock's prophetic and surprisingly spiritual message, remember the Apostle Paul's advice in Philippians: "Finally, brothers and sisters, whatever is true, whatever is noble, whatever is right, whatever is pure, whatever is lovely, whatever is admirable — if anything is excellent or praiseworthy — think about such things…And the God of peace will be with you." (Philippians 4:8-9)

Appendix

Songs, Artists, and Websites containing complete lyrics

Song Title	Artist/band	Lyrics On-line@ www.
Hammer & a Nail	The Indigo Girls	*azlyrics.com/lyrics/indigogirls/ hammerandanail.html*
They Dance Alone	Sting	*seeklyrics.com/lyrics/Sting/They-Dance-Alone.html*
Give a Little Bit	Supertramp	*seeklyrics.com/lyrics/Supertramp/Give-A-Little-Bit.html*
The Ghost of Tom Joad	Bruce Springsteen	*brucespringsteen.net/songs/ TheGhostOfTomJoad.html*
Takin' it to the Streets	The Doobie Brothers	*mp3lyrics.org/d/doobie-brothers/ takin-it-to-the-streets/*
What's Goin' On?	Marvin Gaye	*bluesforpeace.com/lyrics/what's-goin-on.html*
Desperado	The Eagles	*lyricsfreak.com/e/eagles/desperado*
Come Together	The Beatles	*oldielyrics.com/lyrics/the_beatles*
Find the Cost of Freedom	Crosby, Stills, Nash, & Young	*mp3lyrics.org/n/neil-young/find*
Ohio	Crosby, Stills, Nash, & Young	*lyricsdomain.com/14/neil_young/ohio*
Like a Rolling Stone	Bob Dylan	*bobdylan.com/songs/rolling.html*

Song Title	Artist/band	Lyrics On-line@ www.
Born to Run	Bruce Springsteen	lyricsfreak.com/b/bruce+springsteen/born+to+run
Redemption Song	Bob Marley	lyricsfreak.com/b/bob+Marley/redemption+song
Revolution	The Beatles	lyricdepot.com/the-beatles/revolution.html
Roll Me Away	Bob Seger	lyricsdepot.com/bob-seger/roll-me-away.html
The Real Me	The Who	seeklyrics.com/lyrics/The-Who/The-Real-Me.html
What Good am I?	Bob Dylan	bobdylan.com/songs/whatgood.html
The Joker	Steve Miller	metrolyrics.com/the-joker-lyrics-the-steve-miller-band.html
I'm Eighteen	Alice Cooper	lyricsdepot.com/alice-cooper/eighteen.html
What I Am	Edie Brickell	lyricsdownload.com/edie-brickell-what-I-am-lyrics.html
Substitute	The Who	oldielyrics.com/lyrics/the_who/substitute.html
Who are You?	The Who	oldielyrics.com/lyrics/the_who/who_are_you.html
Nowhere Man	The Beatles	seeklyrics.com/lyrics/Beatles/Nowhere-Man.html
Shining Star	Earth, Wind, & Fire	oldielyrics.com/e/earth_wind_and_fire/shining_star.html
As	Stevie Wonder	azlyrics.com/lyrics/steviewonder/as.html
Tin Man	America	oldielyrics.com/lyrics/America/tin_man.html
Message in a Bottle	The Police	seeklyrics.com/lyrics/The-Police/Message-In-A-Bottle.html
Lonely People	America	oldielyrics.com/lyrics/America/lonely_people.html
I Am a Rock	Simon & Garfunkel	mp3lyrics.org/s/simon-garfunkel/I-am-a-rock/

Song Title	Artist/band	Lyrics On-line@ www.
Fire and Rain	James Taylor	mp3lyrics.org/j/james-taylor/fire-and-rain/
Eleanor Rigby	The Beatles	seeklyrics.com/lyrics/Beatles/Eleanor-Rigby.html
Love Song for No One	John Mayer	seeklyrics.com/lyrics/John-Mayer/Love-Song-For-No-One.html
Learn to be Still	The Eagles	azlyrics.com/lyrics/eagles/learntobestill.html
In a New York Minute	The Eagles	azlyrics.com/lyrics/eagles/newyorkminute.html
Secret o' Life	James Taylor	oldielyrics.com/lyrics/james_taylor/secret_o_life.html
59th St. Bridge Song	Simon & Garfunkel	lyricsdepot.com/simon-and-garfunkel/the-59th-street-bridge-song.html
With God on our Side	Bob Dylan	bobdylan.com/songs/withgod.html
American Dream	Crosby, Stills, Nash, & Young	seeklyrics.com/lyrics/Crosby-Stills-Nash-Young/American-Dream.html
Keep on Rockin' in the Free World	Neil Young	azlyrics.com/lyrics/neilyoung/rockininthefreeworld.html
Man in Black	Johnny Cash	azlyrics.com/lyrics/johnnycash/maninblack.html
Dear God	XTC	www.lyricsfreak.com/x/xtc/dear+god_20147941.html
When God Made Me	Neil Young	www.thrasherswheat.org/2005/07/when-god-made-me-lyrics.html
God's Song	Randy Newman	www.lyricsdepot.com/randy-newman/gods-song.html
He Ain't Heavy	The Hollies	oldielyrics.com/lyrics/the_hollies/he_ain't_heavy_hes_my_brother.html
Highway Patrolman	Bruce Springsteen	lyricsdepot.com/bruce-springsteen/highway-patrolman.html

Song Title	Artist/band	Lyrics On-line@ www.
The Heart of the Matter	Don Henley	lyricsdomain.com/4/don_henley/ the_heart_of_the_matter.html
Woodstock	Joni Mitchell	lyricsdir.com/joni-mitchell-woodstock-lyrics.html
Morning Has Broken	Cat Stevens	allspirit.co.uk/morning.html
Goin' to the Country	Bruce Cockburn	lyricsdownload.com/Cockburn-bruce-going-to-the-country-lyrics.html
Beds are Burning	Midnight Oil	anysonglyrics.com/lyrics/m/midnightoil/ beds.html
Amazonia	Stephen Stills	lyricsdepot.com/stephen-stills/amazonia.html
Conviction of the Heart	Kenny Loggins	lyricsdepot.com/kenny-loggins/ conviction-of-the-heart.html
Clear Blue Skies	Crosby, Stills, Nash, & Young	seeklyrics.com/lyrics/Crosby-Stills-Nash-Young/Clear-Blue-Skies.html
Imagine	John Lennon	bluesforpeace.com/lyrics/imagine.html
Turn, Turn, Turn	The Byrds	digitaldreamdoor.com/pages/ music_rm/turn_turn_turn.html
Stop this Train	John Mayer	seeklyrics.com/lyrics/John-Mayer/ Stop-This-Train.html
My Generation	The Who	lyricsdomain.com/20/the_who/ my_generation.html
Hey, Hey, My, My	Neil Young	mp3lyrics.org/n/neil-young/ hey-hey-my-my-into-the-black
Might as Well Have a Good Time	Crosby, Stills, & Nash	lyricsdepot.com/crosby-stills-nash-and-young/ might-as-well-have-a-good-time.html
The Rest of the Night	Warren Zevon	last.fm/music/Warren+Zevon/_/ The+Rest+of+the+Night
Yesterday	The Beatles	lyricsdomain.com/2/beatles/yesterday.html
Sugar Mountain	Neil Young	azlyrics.com/lyrics/neilyoung/ sugarmountain.html

Song Title	Artist/band	Lyrics On-line@ www.
Baby Seat	Barenaked Ladies	azlyrics.com/lyrics/barenakedladies/babyseat.html
Afternoons & Coffeespoons	Crash Test Dummies	azlyrics.com/lyrics/crashtestdummies/afternoonsandcoffeespoons.html
When I'm 64	The Beatles	mp3lyrics.org/b/beatles/when-im-64/
Glory Days	Bruce Springsteen	lyricsdepot.com/bruce-springsteen/glory-days.html
Fred Jones, Part II	Ben Folds	http://info.benfolds.org/FredJonesPart2Lyrics
Still Crazy After All These Years	Paul Simon	lyricsdomain.com/19/simon_garfunkel/still_crazy_after_all_these_years.html
Touch of Grey	Grateful Dead	seeklyrics.com/lyrics/Grateful-Dead/Touch-Of-Grey.html
Keep Me in your Heart	Warren Zevon	seeklyrics.com/lyrics/Warren-Zevon/Keep-Me-In-Your-Heart.html
Alive Again	Chicago	seeklyrics.com/lyrics/Chicago/Alive-Again.html
Spirit in the Sky	Norman Greenbaum	stlyrics.com/lyrics/Michael/spiritinthesky.htm
Here Comes the Sun	The Beatles	seeklyrics.com/lyrics/Beatles-The/Here-Comes-The-Sun.html
New Beginning	Tracy Chapman	seeklyrics.com/lyrics/Trapt/New-Beginning.html
The Rising	Bruce Springsteen	azlyrics.com/lyrics/brucespringsteen/therising.html
Heaven	Los Lonely Boys	azlyrics.com/lyrics.loslonelyboys/heaven.html
Maybe there's a World	Yusuf Islam	lyricsdir.com/yusuf-islam-maybe-theres-a-world-lyrics.html
You Can't Always Get What You Want	The Rolling Stones	keno.org/stones_lyrics/you_can't_always_get_what_you_want.html

Song Title	Artist/band	Lyrics On-line@ www.
I Still Haven't Found What I'm Looking For	U2	azlyrics.com/lyrics/u2/ istillhaventfoundwhatimlookingfor.html
I Can't Get No Satisfaction	The Rolling Stones	keno.org/stones_lyrics/satisfaction.html
Hungry Heart	Bruce Springsteen	lyricsdomain.com/2/bruce_springsteen/ hungry_heart.html
One	U2	lyricstime.com/u2-one-lyrics.html
The Sea Refuses No River	Pete Townshend	mp3lyrics.org/p/pete-townshend/ the-sea-refuses-no-river/
Higher Ground	Stevie Wonder	lyricsdepot.com/stevie-wonder/ higher-ground.html
City of Blinding Lights	U2	azlyrics.com/lyrics/u2/ cityofblindinglights.html
Black and White	Three Dog Night	oldielyrics.com/lyrics/three_dog_night/ black_and_white.html
Get Together	The Youngbloods	stlyrics.com/lyrics/easyrider/gettogether.htm
One Love	Bob Marley	seeklyrics.com/lyrics/Bob-Marley/ One-Love.html
Ebony & Ivory	Paul McCartney/ Stevie Wonder	absolutelyrics.com/lyrics/view/ paul_mccartney/ebony_and_ivory.html
What It's Like	Everlast	lyricsdomain.com/5/everlast/ what_its_like.html
MmMmMm Song	Crash Test Dummies	azlyrics.com/lyrics/crashtestdummies/ mmmmmmmmmmmm.html
Millworker	James Taylor	21lyric.com/J/James-Taylor-lyrics/ Live/Millworker/
Sinaloa Cowboys	Bruce Springsteen	lyricsdepot.com/bruce-springsteen/ sinaloa-cowboys.html
Brick	Ben Folds	lyricsdepot.com/ben-folds-five/brick.html

Song Title	Artist/band	Lyrics On-line@ www.
Marker in the Sand	Pearl Jam	*azlyrics.com/lyrics/pearljam/ markerinthesand.html*
The Times They are a'Changin	Bob Dylan	*bobdylan.com/songs/times.html*

Credits

103